REDEFINING

A Journey to
Finding Yourself,
True Healing and
Spiritual Recalibration

BY PHOENIX WHITE

Hi Kelley,

You Have an amazing mother. I Hope you find some beautiful AHA moments as you read my journey. Let me know what you think

Love

Phoenix White

Acclaim for

REDEFINING

Strong

A Journey to
Finding Yourself,
True Healing and
Spiritual Recalibration

This book is so powerful! Phoenix has penned a text book on life, love, re-demption, gratitude and the eternal search for meaning. Nothing in God's world happens by accident so it is no accident that she has come out the other side stronger and with divine purpose. Take a walk down Phoenix White's yellow brick road and through all the challenges and roadblocks, you, too, will discover that you can go home again, and that, all along, the way home has been through faith.

—— **Pat O'Brien**
Author, Television Host,
Access Hollywood, The Insider, CBS

Phoenix does far more than Redefine Strong in this tale of transparency. She provides a road map for resilience and serves as a guide to never giving up. Phoenix White personifies the term 'Rising from the Ashes.' For all of us stuck in a rut...this is the book that can not only inspire us, but provide direction to healing and redemption.

—— **Jeff Johnson**
Award Winning Journalist, Thought Leader,
MSNBC, BET, Iyanla's 'Fix My Life'.

Copyright

Copyright © 2014 by Phoenix White

First edition: December 2014
The publisher is not responsible for websites (or their content) that are not owned by the publisher.

For author booking, book signings, interviews and events.
Please contact: info@agcreativegroup.com
or visit the authors website: www.phoenixwhite.net

ISBN: 978-0-9912836-1-3 (hard cover)
ISBN: 978-0-9912836-0-6 (paperback)
ISBN: 978-0-9912836-2-0 (e book)

Library of Congress Control Number: 2014920831

AccessGranted
PUBLISHING

Credits

COVER PHOTO
Corey Reese, Corey Reese Photography

MAKEUP
Magen Grays

STYLING
Aja Franks

RETOUCHING
Arina Princess

BOOK DESIGN & LAYOUT:
Phoenix White

Emkron Studios

COPY EDITING
Phoenix White

Emily Claudette Freeman

Caleb Henderson

ADDITIONAL PHOTOGRAPHY:
Corey Reese

DeWayne Rogers

Brandon Lee Anderson

Pierre Conley

Dedication

I dedicate this book to my son, Chimere. I love you more than anyone else in the whole world. You have been my greatest teacher. You are the spark that kept me going when I wanted to give up. Thank you for being connected and compassionate whenever I was having a rough time. For wiping my tears on nights when I tried my best to hide them from you. Thank you for your forgiveness whenever I messed up while I learned how to be a mom. Thank you for leaving me love notes on my pillow at night and telling me that I was doing a great job. Thank you for your kisses in the morning when you thought I was asleep; that meant the world to me. Thank you for riding the waves with mommy even when it got real bumpy and scary, you still trusted me. Thank you for allowing me to sacrifice bits of your time as I worked on this book and being my biggest cheerleader in everything I do. Thank you for loving me, just as I am. You are the Greatest Gift. I wouldn't change it for the world.

Love Always,

- Mommy

Note from the Author

I just wanted to take a moment to say 'Thank You' for simply opening my book to read even the first sentence. This book is the most powerful body of work that I have ever created, and it has literally changed my world in every way. The process itself pushed me to dig deep into the depths of my being to identify the broken places that had been bleeding out into different areas of my life. Only then was I able to do the work & surgery on my broken wings so that I could heal, and ultimately learn how to fly.

Redefining Strong was written solely out of obedience. I heard the whispers in my spirit to write this book many times, but I had no idea what to write or how. But eventually the tugging on my soul became so intense that I could no longer ignore it. I felt that if I didn't do my part that I would be holding up someone else's purpose or ability to move forward. I don't claim to know it all, nor was this book created to proclaim myself as such as I am far from perfect. But what this book will provide is tools for you to use that have helped me to grow into someone that I love without all of the heaviness, shame, guilt and emptiness I had accumulated over time. I've gathered information from many teachers in different shapes, forms, people and experiences. That is what I am offering you through the stories of my journey.

As I've endured being torn from my family and unjustifiably placed in a foster home as a child, to my battle with depression, abuse, heartache, rape, and suicide attempts; to being thrown in jail facing prison time. Not to mention, the process of surviving brain surgery, media scrutiny, homelessness & welfare with my child. I'm now finding and living my life on purpose; healing from the inside out and being led by spirit to the most incredible experiences and opportunities I never imagined or even thought possible. It seemed just as I was at the brink of completely giving up, and feeling as if I had accumulated all the pieces to fail. I began to rise from the ashes.

I wanted to write a book that was 100% honest. No sugar coating, just raw untampered with stories, and learning lessons. This book will challenge you to do the work that will open you up to different layers of your being. It will show you how to heal, grow, and shift into alignment so that your life can flow abundantly with purpose and clarity.

My mission was to share my personal truth and journey to be used as a catalyst to help others to heal, and become empowered to live their best lives. I believe the truth is the only real way to make an impact in the lives of others and most importantly, ourselves. So, I'm ready. I'm no longer afraid of that truth or my past as it has made me who I am.

And you know what, I'm really digging my new self. But it took me quite some time to get there and a lot of inner work. But, I hope to help you speed up the process with the tools that I've gathered over time.

I thank God for giving me the courage and discipline to write this book. I hope that it touches your life as it has mine. Thank you for trusting me to share the knowledge that I have learned, and for opening your minds and hearts as I share with you my very first book. *Redefining Strong.*

With Love,

Phix White

Foreword

BY LAMMAN RUCKER

Friend. Daughter. Sister. Mother. Dreamer. Lover. Giver. Healer. Producer. Singer. Songwriter. Photographer. Graphic Designer. Entrepreneur. Competitor. Fighter. Survivor. Warrior. Winner.

These are merely a few of the words that I can personally use to describe Phoenix White, but the list goes on. It was over ten years ago when we met by chance and have become like family in the years since. Throughout that time, I've been able to witness a transformation unlike many I've ever seen before. I've seen her shaken and stirred; vision blinded and blurred. I've seen her spirit hopeful and heroic; also bruised and burned. I've witnessed her magnetism and magnificence; her failures and fears. What I've seen, felt and been inspired by more than anything though, is her ability - like the Phoenix that she is - to rise up and be reborn, forged by fire and flame.

IF anyone knows what it means to be STRONG, it is this woman! This book is not only a shining testament to the wonderful growth and ascension she is experiencing at this time in her own life, but more importantly, it's an opportunity to share with you what her journey is so that it may empower and catapult you into your own paradigm shift and begin to love yourself greater than you did before.

In her light, I now define S.T.R.O.N.G. as the powerful combination of Spirituality, Truth, Resilience, Optimism, Never Giving Up and Gratitude! The more vital definition, however, will come from you! Just as her example and this book have both done for me, I'm certain you will be moved.

Throughout my travels around the world, my many years of teaching, the joys and pains of parenting, the countless hours of family counseling and crisis intervention I've done, the growing number of motivational speeches I've given and the on-going challenges, tribulations and celebrations in my own life. I've come to understand one common denominator in the road to fulfillment and personal power: SELF-LOVE. Without it, self-sabotage, stagnation and shame dominate you.

Make the commitment today - starting now - that any previous patterns of negativity don't have a place in your life any longer. Break the cycle. Choose love. Claim victory. Stand tall. Remind yourself that you are Worthy. Significant. Valuable...And have Purpose.

BELIEVE IT.
PROCLAIM IT.
ACT ON IT.
ACTUALIZE IT.

Arise from the ashes and fly high. You are STRONG. It's time. Love and Light,

~Lamman Rucker
Actor, Activist, Motivational Speaker

CONTENTS

The Invitation

REDEFINING STRONG

FOR many years, I carried a heavy amount of bitterness and hurt that I convinced myself I'd moved past. I suppose, I was incapable or too immature at the time to recognize and acknowledge that it was still a big part of me because a lot of it had happened so long ago. I consistently used the phrase, "I'm over it," but I wasn't. I was just coping with it the best way I knew how. Aside from the fact, no one had ever taught me how to heal. "Just fall on your knee's and pray" was the only advice I ever really got. But that wasn't enough for me. I would frequently grow irritable when people would say things like "you just gotta let it go." I wanted to sarcastically scream, "You let it go! "Stop telling me what to do and start showing me how to do it. Give me an example or shut up; I'm doing the best I can!" Plus, what does that even mean, "Let it Go?" Those were my thoughts for years. I'm sure I'm not the only one that's ever felt that way, as I plowed through doing the work on myself that was required; in order to move forward in my life.

Over the course of the last few years, I began some serious spiritual surgery. I started learning how to cleanse my spirit, cut spiritual cords with people that were still affecting me, and find ways to identify and release left over pieces of the sharp painful glass that had been embedded into my soul. I've come across a few methods that worked for me, and throughout the course of this book, I'm going to share a few of them with you.

At just 34, I have been through much more than one may think. It's funny how at first glance I use to be extremely judged even before the first hello, and treated accordingly. I would often have many people say "I thought you were just one of those stuck up pretty girls that ain't never been through nothing." Simply because I spoke well and made sure I was put together before leaving the house, even if my account is at a zero balance. But many people don't know me! They know of me. I honestly feel as if I've lived many lives in this lifetime, yet I also feel as if it's just begun. So, I invite you to pull up a chair and get ready to dig into my testimony.

Now, there will be some who actually do know me that will read this book and discover many things for the first time. And for some, it may make you a bit uncomfortable but the intention is not to hurt anyone, this is just my truth and my honest reflection. Hopefully you see my heart and use this as an opportunity to reflect, heal and flourish as vulnerable as it may seem. I personally have a hard time listening to people tell me what to do, when they haven't walked in my shoes. That is why I've chosen to open the doors to my closet full of skeletons; so that you will know, I'm no different, no better - I am just like you.

Chapter One

MOMENTS

Every now and then, I have what I like to call 'a moment.' I use to think it was indicative of being weak because I would never cry or be caught doing so. If I did, I would barricade myself in the bathroom, have my mini meltdown, then come out as if nothing had ever happened. I was convinced not expressing my emotions was my way of showing that I was strong, and I could handle everything, but boy was I wrong. As I got older I realized that I just kept all of that stuff bottled up inside of me with no real release until I eventually started to implode.

I remember my days paying for storage and constantly

taking boxes with loads of stuff year after year, stacking it one on top of the other. I kept stuffing it to capacity until one day; nothing else fit and things started toppling over, falling on me, breaking, just pouring out of the boxes like an avalanche. I had so much junk that the foundation I had created became unstable and ultimately fell apart. I was then forced to rummage through this mountain of debris I had collected over time. Only in that moment did I start to ask myself, "what can I get rid of?" I had no other option. But honestly over 90% of it could go.

Think about how much you've paid over the years for stuff you don't need and will never use again because it's time has expired. Whether it's relationships, memories, things, clothes you can't fit that are now outdated, even random pictures and artifacts that belonged to someone else. You just can't seem to let go of it. Yet, it no longer serves you. So why are you holding on to it? At some point, you must make the hard decision to get rid of the debris you're holding hostage. Only then will you in fact become free. But let me warn you, it's a lot of work in every area of your life.

There are moments when sometimes you need to just cry. You've been suppressing it long enough. It's your body's natural way of detoxifying and purging the soul. Once you do, you can release a lot of that hurt, sadness, anger, regret, pain and frustration so that you can get back up feeling a lot lighter. It's ok to just let it out. We have to learn to stop fighting against what our bodies naturally want to do to regain balance and composure.

Most people don't know this about me, but I have self-realization moments all the time and just start crying. Because that's what my body and spirit need. Gone are the days of me choking on my tears in an effort to show others as well as myself that I'm tough and not phased by anything. So I take my moment which usually lasts for about ten minutes or so. Now, this doesn't mean go into depression mode LOL, or start judging your life as a whole. But you have to let whatever you feel pass through you, or it is highly likely to get trapped IN you. I then take a few cleansing breaths, inhaling and exhaling deep and loud. I wipe my tears, lift my head up, and acknowledge the lesson I learned through that experience or truth I now accept as a result of whatever I had come out of. Afterwards, I smile because I learned something, and I'm proud of myself for having the courage to admit my mistakes, recognize when I'm hurt and simply be real with me.

So if you're ready to face yourself so that you can stop paying the price for all of this old stuff you don't need in your life anymore. If you're honestly ready to heal, put in the work and willing to make the sacrifices so that you can finally begin live and experience fulfillment, joy, love and real peace. Let's grab some garbage bags, a few tissues and something to write with so that we can dig this stuff out together.

YOU

can't acknowledge what
you don't accept, and you
can't accept what you
don't identify .

Chapter Two

BITTER BEGINNINGS

When I was a child, I was sent to a foster home along with my two younger sisters. I still remember the police coming to our home as I sat in my room and began hearing some sort of scuffle in the hallway. I heard my mom (whom officers were detaining) screaming, "YOU CAN'T TAKE MY CHILDREN!" Over and over.

I remember like it was yesterday; sitting in the back of a police car with my sisters who were whaling at the top of their lungs, with tears of fear pouring down their faces. But not me, I sat there in silence, as everything seemed to be moving in slow motion. I would later realize that this was a spiritual gift I had when something life changing was happening; everything slows down so that I'm able to take mental snapshots and process every second of it. In actuality, my brain was just processing at a very fast speed. I was confused about why this was happening yet very aware; refusing to cry.

I also recall the moment that I looked out the back window at my mom, which from my memory looks like a slowed down dramatic scene from a movie with music and all; as the officer closed the door and slowly turned on the engine. I remember looking back at my mother who seemed to be hyperventilating in pure panic mode. I'm sure it was out of fear of not knowing what was happening and feeling completely helpless because there was nothing she could do. I then quietly turned around and put my arms around my siblings in an effort to comfort and calm them; as the police car carrying us pulled out of the driveway. What seemed like a normal beautiful sunny day turned into a huge scar that started a wave of resentment and bitterness that would run throughout the course of my life. I was only eight.

After becoming an adult I realized there were a lot of holes in the story of my childhood, and I started doing some digging into my past. I began to ask questions about family secrets that were swept under the rug for so long that it no longer seemed to exist. I was able to piece together the story that led to the moment when my sisters and I were unjustly torn from our family and placed in a foster home.

From what I was told, it all started when I was taken to the doctor because I had hurt myself on a bike. This injury had caused my vagina to hurt extremely bad. I remember this day because I was riding a boy's bike with the bar down the center and I wasn't able to touch the ground because I was too short, and somehow I came down really hard on that bar in an effort to stop the bike. It was some of the worst pain I have ever felt. That innocent day turned into a huge court battle with my parents because I allegedly contracted Chlamydia at eight years old which is what the doctors I suppose stated during my visit. How? Honestly, I have no idea. It blows my mind still to this day. Needless to say, I never even knew about that part until I was well into my 20's. Nor do I have any traumatic memories of how I could have contracted it. It was as if it was wiped from my memory. Or, it just simply never happened.

My family never spoke about the whole situation regarding the STD that was presumably contracted from my father (This was later proven incredibly false.) I believe this presumption was because I was the closest to my dad. But he had never done anything like that to me ever. Not to mention the 'questionable' test results magically just disappeared during trial.

I STILL have memories of sitting in a child psychologist's office while she pointed to different parts of a gingerbread doll asking me if my daddy touched me here or there. I felt like they were trying to convince me of something, no matter how many times I would honestly reply no. Either way; this incident tore my family apart, and I was at the core of it. Even then, it seemed like this dark energy was out to destroy me from the very beginning of my life. It was always something.

The irony of this whole thing about my dad is that he wouldn't even dry us off when we got out the bath. He would always throw this huge towel between our legs so that his hands never touched us, ever. All of my sisters can attest to that. I had to wash my sisters up. He said; that was something my grandmother taught him, "never touch your girls down there." My dad was still arrested, thrown in jail, treated like a horrible criminal and discharged from the navy temporarily. He also wasn't allowed to see us (his kids) and had to move out of our house in order for us to come home from foster care; once they were able to find us, while his friends and our neighbors ridiculed him for a crime he didn't commit. That event single-handedly destroyed my entire family, and I was to blame at the center of it all. Even though at the time I didn't understand why. I've always felt bad about that; because my father is a great dad who loves his children, has never abandoned any of us, and is one of my best friends.

During the time away from our parents, my sisters and I ended up in two separate foster homes which I hated more than anything. My younger sister Jenea and I stayed at the same place, and we made the foster mom's life hell. We would purposely scream and cry at the top of our lungs every night; as we laid in a dark room that resembled a creepy triangular attic. I will never forget the circular window that faced an old tree outside. It seemed to always catch the moonlight just enough to create a creepy shadow on the wall at night as the limbs waved from side to side in the wind. I will also never forget catching the foster mom sneaking purple and red medicine into our oatmeal, which is why I don't eat it to this day. I always thought she was trying to drug my sister and I. So I became very quiet and withdrawn. Never speaking. Never playing with the other kids. Just sitting and watching everyone; waiting for my parents to rescue me from what I called the wicked witch.

When my sisters and I were finally allowed to go back home, it seemed as if we were immediately sent off to Texas to be with our grandfather; for what was suppose to be a summer vacation. Our grandfather was a man we had never met before; nor had we ever seen a picture of; or even heard about him at all for that matter.

Since my mother was of a lighter skin color with silky curly hair and very well spoken; my assumption was that we were going to a place straight out of the TV show 'DALLAS.'

Filled with sunny days, big ranches and beautiful horses. That was the only thing that came to mind when I thought of Texas. I was so excited to meet my new grandpa. Whom in my head, was a white man with a big cowboy hat and a southern accent. To this day I still have no idea why on earth I thought that. But I did.

IF

you don't transform from
your pain. Then it was for
nothing .

Chapter Three

THE SCARLET LETTER

From the moment my sister and I got off the plane; we saw this enormous overweight black man waiting for us. He had an extremely greasy looking jheri curl, sweating profusely as if he had run a marathon, with his stomach grotesquely bulging out from under his shirt saying he was our grandfather. I immediately became protective, grabbed my little sisters hand from him and told the flight attendants that we didn't know him. He was furious as he was sent away to get his id. I hoped with all my heart that he wasn't the man who we had to live with, and that they would send us back home. But he was. I was upset and confused as I sat quietly during the 3-hour drive into the woods anxiously waiting to see a beautiful ranch magically pop up somewhere. We finally arrived; after turning off onto a long dirt road to an old, rundown, small, dark, creepy house with no working toilets in the middle of nowhere. I thought, this couldn't be real, but it was. Hell, the first week we were there my grandfather was beating us with hand size branches with leaves (not switches) because we wouldn't eat sardines. Seriously, what child do you know of that sits around eating sardines? We were from California! Needless to say, we were beat like slaves for wasting "his food" and had to go outside in the middle of the night to use the bathroom.

I was angry and confused as to why we were sent to what seemed like such a God forsaken place. I did chores that I had never heard of in my life. For instance; weed hacking 6 ft high plants growing off to the side of the yard that looked similar to a duck pond that was filled with actual sewage that came up to our knees and frequently spilled over into our rubber boots. Mowing huge lawns that took almost two days to complete nothing about it was a vacation.

While waiting for this summer from hell to be over anger and bitterness began to grow in me. I was tired of the way he was treating us. So one day, when my grandfather went to work, I packed my sister and I's stuff and dragged our broken suitcases up the rocky dirt road to an aunt's house we had met a few days prior who seemed so nice. Plus, she had young daughters in their 20's that were married living on the property in separate trailer homes. So when my grandfather came home, we were nowhere to be found, and refused to go back.

A few weeks after arriving at my great aunts house, I was told in front of everybody, that we were sent there because my dad had done sexual stuff to me and that I liked it! I was told they knew this apparently, because my five-year-old sister said she saw it; meanwhile, she had no idea what they were talking about, but she said yes because they told her to. I asked myself; Where did this information come from? Was it my mother? I remember feeling like I was being choked by my tears as I tried to control them from pouring down my face.

As I sat in the middle of a room with all of these people that I didn't know; having this so called factual conversation about me while I filled with so much shame, even though I knew it wasn't true.

When I tried to defend myself I was told to shut up and stop trying to take up for my dad and that I was "fast," which by cultural definition, meant a whore. So I was labeled a whore for all to scoff and judge at eight years old by people who knew nothing about me. Yet, they were supposedly my family; as the news spread like wildfire because they had nothing else to do but gossip.

Now, did I grow to love them over time? Of course, but I was still a bit distant as I began to carry the shame of something that never happened. As well as the guilt for being the sole reason, we were taken away from our family. Engraved in my mind was simply that it was all my fault.

What we were told was going to be a short summer, ended up being a year that turned into two years. I felt unwanted and forgotten. I would dream about how I could run away without getting lost or hurt in the woods that surrounded the trailer house on all four sides. I would even promise my sister I would come back for her as I plotted my escape each night or as I prayed to be rescued.

When my dad finally got back home, I'm assuming after everything was cleared up, he sent for us. But as soon as he went to sea again, my mom sent us back to Texas. I didn't understand that as a child because although she sent us clothes, or paid for stuff (as she expressed, which by the way I knew nothing about), I didn't feel loved. I felt abandoned. It was only recently as an adult and through gathering information for this book; that I found out how all hell had broken loose between my mother and father. I didn't know she was doing the best she could and had no way to care for us at the time. But that was never communicated to us. I don't remember being told anything at all. Ever. I don't even remember speaking to my mother much. I only recently found out that my mother use to call all the time, but she was told we were unavailable. Even when she would send money and gifts, they always told us it was them that had bought the items. Or when she would send us money, we never received it or knew anything about it. I never knew as a kid that these people kept my parents at bay while constantly reiterating that they do nothing for us. I would always say, my dad is coming to get me, and they would just laugh and say "child your dad ain't thinking about you," as if we were thrown out and unwanted. They constantly made me feel like I owed them something, well into my adulthood.

How did this affect me as I grew up? I was very quiet, never feeling deserving or good enough. I allowed people to place whatever title they came up with on me, and I never defended myself. I never believed anyone would listen even if I did.

During elementary and junior high school I began to be bullied by girls and targeted by boys. They would hit me, push me down, slap me, call me names, pull my hair out, spread rumors and whatever else came to mind. I would let people say or do whatever to me, and I would just be silent. I ran from confrontation because I didn't want to cause more drama or pain. I didn't believe I had a voice. My only outlet was when I sang or wrote in one of my many journals.

I remember when my parents began to fight over who's turn it was to keep us. Sometimes my sister Jenea and I would have to keep our bags packed because my parents would drop us off two or three times in one night because the other was mad that it wasn't their turn. It left us feeling irrelevant most times. When in actuality they were just angry and bitter with one another.

As an adult, I would always think my relationships would end in me being abandoned whether it was serious or not, and that is exactly what always seemed to happen. I constantly felt I wasn't enough. It was my fault no matter how much of myself I gave; or that something was wrong with me.

Remember when I said that I was placed in a foster home because I had supposedly contracted an STD at 8? Well, every serious boyfriend I have ever loved which only consisted of about 3, all of them gave me a std (sexually transmitted disease) at one time or another. I eventually forgave them all. But it was like a curse of the ages. I felt I couldn't trust anyone. Love to me was also automatic pain. I have always had a strange way of forgiving and loving people no matter what. Forgiving them came so easily it almost seemed surreal to me and them honestly. But at the time I didn't know any better. They all seemed so sad that they had hurt me. I was naive as hell, but that's the truth. I trusted the people I loved even when they gave me plenty of reasons not to. So in retrospect, I'm partly responsible for allowing it, when I should have known better, yet I consistently chose to ignore the signs I was given, because I so badly craved to be wanted.

AT one point in my life, it seemed people were always looking to tragically hurt me somehow. Heartache and disappoint seemed to follow me everywhere I went.

My first sexual experience was at 16 with a guy I had the biggest crush on; which painfully turned out to be a bet between him and his friends. My first time was nothing more than a ridiculous bet amongst boys! That devastated me. Again, I was labeled, scoffed at and ridiculed as it spread throughout the school. In my eyes sex was awful, I didn't like it at all. There was nothing beautiful about it. It didn't even last 5 minutes because it hurt so bad. But still, to think he was only nice to me to take my virginity as a bet; hurt even more. And to make matters worse, he never even talked to me again, and that crushed me.

Now, even though that was my first time having sex, and I never did it again until I was 18; I was stamped once again with the scarlet letter as something I wasn't. The cycle had continued from when I was 8 and I was so ashamed. But yet again; in my mind, I had no voice to defend myself. To me, no one would care anyway.

Even on a night as important and special as my graduation night, as all of my family came down for what appeared more like a family reunion for them, more so than a celebration for me. It seemed no one barely even talked to or paid me much attention. Although I was being filmed the entire day by the local news station for being the most inspirational student in all of San Diego. I had broke educational records and challenged the school laws that they believed were scholastically and physically unattainable by finishing a year's worth of work for seven classes in one week. I was so proud, but I felt no one cared but my grandmother. It was like I wasn't even there.

SO that night, a guy I had met previously as a pizza delivery boy, who was also a popular promoter invited me to a party he was throwing. He picked me up from my house, and I had a great time. I was all VIP and feeling special. But after the party; he wouldn't take me home. He said he had to stop at his house, which was filled with guys somewhere around 15 of them, no girls. I remember feeling so uncomfortable as I sat frozen in one spot while the guys looked at me like I was a piece of steak in a lions den. They were drunk and the house was filled with weed smoke. I remember feeling so exhausted as I kept asking him to please take me back to my house where he had picked me up.

It was around 3 am and I was becoming afraid and rightfully so. That night, he eventually ended up raping me through anal sex. It felt like a knife ripping through me as he pressed my head into the side of the bed that he had forcefully bent me over, and lifted my navy blue dress. It seemed to all happen within seconds. I remember being so outwardly calm as I was crying quietly and shivering in pain after every quick stab he made as he entered into my body, while I softly pleaded, "please let me go." All of this took place while his friends were laughing and trying to film it from up above the low loft like wall that peered over into the room. I was so embarrassed, so ashamed, and hurting from the inside out.

Needless to say; he never took me home because he didn't 'feel like it.' He was angry for some reason and had one of his boys drop me off at the bus station at the corner, and I had to walk the rest of the way at 6am. I finally got to my house sore, exhausted, with an itchy burning sensation from being ripped quite a bit and bleeding a little underneath my dress. I remember my family being angry with me for not coming home. But I didn't really believe they cared or even noticed I was gone, as well as I was too drained and ashamed to tell them where I was and what had happened. So I lived with that secret for many years until now. I began to detach myself from sex. It was never something I found to be pleasurable in my earlier years; it was just something everyone wanted from me. That is the only way they saw me; I didn't exist otherwise.

The effects of labels, mis-use, abuse and rape trickled into my adult life. Naively, I met and became involved with men whom I thought were great and really wanted me. Only to discover I was merely someone they wanted to conquer; and many times they would just take it from me. I was left bearing the weight of shame and feeling responsible for being in the wrong places at the wrong times. My access to luxuries like hanging out in major recording studios; writing songs with some of the top producers in the world, or working toward my dream of being a singer was restricted or cut off entirely. If I didn't act like I was in to them in some way, I seemingly missed out on many of what I thought were opportunities at the time by refusing to do a lot of what was propositioned; if weren't actually stolen from me.

There were many times; actually most times if I'm keeping it all the way real. I felt that I had to have sex with someone because if I didn't they would hurt me in some way. Or because I was there alone with these men and there was no way out other than to give them what they wanted. So I went with it, consciously trying my best to not make them upset, hoping to hurry up and get it over with. Because in my mind, I was afraid they would take it anyway or do something mean and drastic. Even if that weren't the case, that was my fear.

Then there were also times that the men I encountered were so powerful; that if I didn't do what they asked or propositioned they would threaten to ruin my career before it was even started. I honestly never felt NO was a real option in the world of powerful men. Aside from the fact that I was literally terrified because whenever I said no, they would make me feel so bad as if my presence had done something to provoke their aggressive behavior. I would allow myself to feel bad, like I was wrong, and would use the sex they wanted to make up for my seemingly bad behavior in some twisted sick way.

Even though, I knew I had done nothing wrong. Their resentment, tone, and probable rage made me uncomfortable and nervous; as I did everything I could to reverse that anger into the passionate sex they wanted. Which I somehow begin to transmute in to love and care. Funny thing is, at that time in my life I didn't even like sex. I wasn't even comfortable enough with my body to even take all my clothes off in front of someone. I didn't feel beautiful, or sexy like they did in the movies. I didn't feel safe, nor did I have any idea what I was doing. It was almost as if it became an act as I barely ever had any real orgasmic experiences. I was numb and had disconnected myself from embracing the true beauty and spiritual nature of what sex actually was.

O ver time, I began to feel like no one cared about my brain or how smart and talented I was, or if I had feelings or not. That cold pain became normal for me. I unconsciously began looking for someone to just want ME, which in return made me a target to be manipulated easily. From the age of 8 through my late 20's, bitterness, pain and disappointment became my constant companion.

If all of that wasn't bad enough, I had found myself in the midst of what probably would be a script for a reality show. A relationship with someone I loved more than anyone turned into a huge painful media scandal. All because I trusted and fell in love with the wrong person. One who wouldn't just simply stand up for what was right. So, once again, I was being stamped, ridiculed and accused of doing and being something that wasn't true. And once again, I felt I had no voice to defend myself. I believed saying something would only make things worse. Meanwhile the safety of silence ultimately became my form of protection. As well as an exhausting weight that I continued to drag around limiting me from being able to move forward. I endured so much during that time and I eventually became very sick. I couldn't hold on to my weight and went from a size 13 or 32 in jeans to a size 0 or 20. I was fluctuating between 90-102 pounds. I was so skinny, and so not sexy. My family was terrified for me, questioning if I had caught aids or something similar; but I was just depressed.

I started having week-long headaches and buzzing in my

ear that would result in me randomly losing consciousness throughout the day. Which eventually led me to having brain surgery. The stress and pain from many years of hurt that I had trapped inside was literally killing me.

NOT too long ago, I decided that I would change the story that I had been telling myself all those years. I decided to no longer be a victim, or carry the weight and responsibility of someone else's insecurities or thirst for power and acceptance. I chose to release myself and muster up the courage to allow my broken spirit to heal. And yes, it does take courage. Courage to embrace the lessons in all of my experiences, instead of finding someone to blame. And there, while in the midst of it all, I found my voice. I suddenly realized that being vulnerable and honest enough to share my feelings with others instead of acting as if I didn't care was real strength. I discovered that when I concealed and masked my pain, I was still living a life controlled, ashamed & still affected by the turmoil of it all, which was a heavy burden to bare.

My world was similar to that of having a gorgeous house with freshly mowed green grass that people drive by and are so jealous of. A house with dark curtains covering the windows that I was too afraid to open because my house was filled with an enormous amount of old garbage. Much of which had been thrown in by myself and others and left rotting inside for years. So, I decided to clean out my house - my spirit, and my heart; and it took a lot of work, but it has been the best decision I've ever made in my life. I now have an inner peace and calm to my soul that I have never experienced before. How did I get there? Well, I'm going to show you.

Soul Exercise

DAMAGE REPORT

A damage report is something that I came up with that allows me to look at my past and compare it to my present. It helps you to figure out where certain issues or damaging habits you have stem from. In order to do this, you have to be brutally honest with yourself in identifying the issues. So, if you're ready, we can head over to the next step. If not, take your time and come back to it.

This exercise is simply for you to identify where some of these issues come from. That way once you acknowledge what they are, you can begin to be aware of them and catch yourself. That way you can start working to heal that area, promoting change.

L et's start with just **3** things you want to change. It can be something as simple as drinking too much alcohol, or being easily angered and having a quick temper, being overly possessive, needy or insecure. Think about what the triggers are? Where do you think this stemmed from?

THEY
tried to bury us, but
they didn't know we
were seeds.

-Mexican Proverb

Soul Exercise

What's the Issue?

Make sure to write down things you really want to change about yourself that have become a hindrance to you making progress in your life.

be *honest*

keep it short and to the point. #NoJudgement

What Triggers the Issue?

What happens that makes you resort to the main issue?
Do you get stressed, afraid, lonely, bored? Think about it.

Damage Report

I have an issue with...

_____

_____

_____

_____

_____

_____

Everytime I feel...

_____

_____

_____

_____

_____

_____

I started doing this after...

_____

_____

_____

_____

_____

When did this issue start?

What event in your life happened that prompted this to start?

NO
EXCUSES
KEEP

Going

I will start..

_____

_____

_____

_____

_____

_____

What steps can you take to change it?

Chapter Four

THE MORNING AFTER

O ne day, I woke up inspired and ready to just grow up. Life happens in phases and levels. We all experience key turning points in that force us to make a decision to go one-way, or another. You can choose to go forward, backward, or stay stuck where you are. I decided that it was time to make some real drastic changes in my world as I entered into the next stage of my journey.

Journal Entry: February 12, 2013

I saw a vision of myself today balled up in a dark corner, hiding as if I was in a box nestled in what looked to be a cave of concrete and debris. I was cowering after multiple massive tornadoes hit my life and my world.

My head was tucked down as my arms covered over the top, when I heard a soft voice say, "You can come out now. It's ok; you made it don't be afraid."

I could see echoing rays from the sun shooting through the rubble while pieces of rock and dirt fell to the ground as I began to move around carefully. I squinted, as a small beam of bright light started to burn my eyes slightly since being in the dark for so long. I was fatigued; with very little strength, but I was moving. It had taken me quite a while to come outside. You see, I'd found some sense of comfort in my small dark hole. I had begun to feel safe there.

I made my way outside and was a bit taken aback. There in front of me was the most beautifully cut green grass while soft, dewy drops glistened as they settled upon it. The golden glow of the rising sun danced as it peeked through the trees in the distance as I closed my eyes and took a deep breath. The fresh air felt so good and crisp; it seemed to be rushing through my body cleansing and restarting my internal computer. For so long it seemed I was powered off. I had lost my way and my true sense of self. Sometimes you just start to malfunction; as you become overwhelmed trying to process so much that you just freeze up and you need to be shut down and often unplugged.

It was the first time in a long time I felt clear, calm, free; there was nothing but me. The real me. As the warmth of the sun caressed my skin, I stood there frozen. It was so beautiful for miles, just flat land filled with vibrant green grass while the trees stood tall with confidence in pure silence, bliss. I started to walk feeling the wet, cool grass between my toes. But for some reason I was compelled to stop and turn around to see where I had come from, to see what I was leaving behind me.

I caught a glimpse as I began to turn and dropped to my knees. It seemed everything had been destroyed. There were miles and miles of destruction and rubble. I covered my mouth in an attempt to stop myself from screaming as I began to feel the heat of my tears rushing down my face.

It was then that everything began to hurt as I realized I had cuts, bruises and swelling everywhere. All of a sudden; it became harder to breathe, as if my ribs were even broken. I just wanted to crawl back into my hole. The pain was so overwhelming. It hurt so badly. I thought, "There is no way I can salvage or fix any of this!" I didn't have it in me. Everything was gone! Everyone was gone. My pride hurt. My heart ached. My spirit was broken. I felt as if everything was taken from me.

For years, it seemed I allowed people to steal pieces of my essence & soul. Or, maybe I just naively gave it away, until the foundation of who I was became so weak that my world came crashing down. I was devastated. But then I heard that same soft voice again, "You don't need any of this, everything you need is in you. Turn around, Leave it where it is, look at what is in front of you, not what is behind." My spirit continued to whisper, "You will feel so much better when you're looking forward, it only hurts when you're looking back; turnaround." The voice whispered, "see all of that beauty in front of you? Leave that stuff where it is. Don't take any of it, let it go."

AT that moment, I had what Oprah would call an 'Aha moment,' revelation began rushing through me like a shot of morphine. "I get it," I said to myself. Most of what had been taken away had been the cause of most of my pain, turmoil and hurt. I had to leave it all in order for there to be any real change. My world had been destroyed; as many things and many people had been taken away in a vicious, painful manner. But it had to happen that way; otherwise I would just keep letting those people back in, hurting myself, changing the course of my future. I often wondered why I kept doing that, other than I loved them. At least that is what I convinced myself of, as most people do. Even though, things weren't so great. I guess I thought it would get better. I could settle for it because I figured there is no perfect love. Or either; who I thought I was; had been lost over the course of years trying to please others while changing myself. I do know that when it comes to relationships, often people do what you allow. That was definitely the case in my past relationships. Usually, former loves expected to be let back into my heart, and my life if they just gave things a little time.

THE
painful reality is; they were not afraid to hurt me, abuse my trust, lie on me, or to me, because they were never really afraid to lose me. I had given so much of myself to people who didn't deserve me. Because I was unaware of what I deserved. I was constantly let down, and continually taking them back based on temporary heartfelt, I'm sorry's, and I love

you's that never seemed to last longer than a few months, sometimes weeks. There were no real consequences, no real love, no real respect, and no real loyalty.

Most of them were only around when they needed something or they were lonely and needed affection & love to build them up; while depleting me. Then after they got it, they left. They often patched me up with typical excuses of it's not you, it's me. Or the ever so famous 'I don't want to hurt you' line. Many people in my life didn't just give, just because they loved me. I take that back, there were some incredible men in my life as I got older that sometimes did. But I realized I loved the people I dated way more than myself. I sacrificed my happiness, because I never knew I deserved it; which led me to making permanent decisions with people who were temporary. I played a big part in my own destruction because I didn't know what it meant to truly be loved, not even by myself.

Like many of you, I subconsciously thought that pain was

a version of love. I had a huge tolerance for this because my father was quite abusive when I was younger. I don't want to hurt his feelings because he was a great dad and still is. He was always there whenever I needed him, never abandoned us and took very good care of his kids. But he had a violent temper; especially when he was drinking and pissed off with my mom. He beat the hell out of us for the slightest things that were bad, as most black parents do. A butt spanking is considered the norm.

When he calmed down, he would feel extremely bad and precede to tell us that he loved us. We were treated hard like boys. I'm sure part of it was due to his being falsely accused during the whole molestation case. He disconnected from being gentle in many areas; even his hugs were rough. But after doing a little investigating, I discovered that my dad's father was exactly the same. That is what he was taught. He knew no other way to actually communicate his anger. He, like many parents, did the best he could with the tools he was given. I don't condone it, but I'm way more compassionate when I think about it as I travel on this journey of healing and forgiveness. He's come a long way since then. He's barely the same person, he's older now and more at peace, loving and way more gentle in his approach to everything, and I'm very proud of him for always striving to be and do better.

But with that being my experience, my tolerance for abuse was way higher than it's supposed to be. As well as my odd understanding of a man's lack of care, gentleness, and shortage of affection for me was all skewed in my mind. At one time, I had convinced myself that I didn't need any of that. Not even a real commitment, title or outward acknowledgment; as I continued to be faithful and patient to men who were emotionally unavailable or abusive to me, and I nicknamed it a relationship. I however began attributing pain & heartache to love up until the age of 31. As I convinced myself that strength was being able to take it and not break.

I allowed people to unleash their irresponsible, abusive behavior on me, which subsequently left me blaming myself for the hurt they had caused. I was even afraid to hold them accountable because I feared they would leave me. But in the end, they left anyway.

I realized after I allowed them to take all of their inner conflict, confusion and past pain out on me; I was the one left carrying a weight that was never mine to begin with. I wasn't aware of my own self-value. It never occurred to me, that I in fact needed to be cared for; as much as I cared for others. I found that I had a hard time leaving people because I knew what it was like to be abandoned, and I didn't want to hurt anyone like that. So, I endured and kept quiet; as I was consistently run over and left to glue together the broken pieces. I was a magnet for broken men. I gave to them the unconditional love, loyalty, patience, support and care that I in fact, needed. Only for them to end up with someone else, yet always stating how much they love me, even now.

ONE DAY I decided none of that was okay

anymore. It wasn't normal. I started having a real conversation with myself. There are actually some amazing, beautiful people who wanted to be in my life. I thought, "what am I doing? Is this what I really want?" Or just what I'm settling for because I've somehow found a way to make my dysfunctional relationships with people functional. I unconsciously wanted to save them in the same ways I needed to be saved in order to fill my own gaping wound. Or; maybe somehow I felt validated by cultural standards by having someone, anyone. Whatever the case, I began to realize this couldn't be love. And even if it were, it wasn't what I honestly wanted. So I began to do something that I had never actually done. I got up the courage to stand up for myself.

I was completely aware that I would lose many people as I began to find my voice and rationally express what I needed as a woman, a human being and what I wouldn't tolerate. No longer would I allow being disrespected, lied on, or get use to someone's lack of respect for my time and effort. I found the balls to be okay with walking away, even if that meant I had to cry all day afterward.

Walking away from something you have grown accustomed to for years or someone you've loved for what seems like forever, whether it was good or bad, hurts like hell. There is no easy way out of it. Yet, there's nothing worse than staying stuck in a place where you're not supposed to be.

Many times we are in relationships that leave us stuck in every area of our lives, but as soon as we leave – the chains come off. Life becomes so clear almost in an instant. Once we allow ourselves to see it, we often realize we were sitting there with the key the whole time. Honestly it's not that those we love are bad people; they are just not good for us anymore.

Soul Exercise

• Take a moment and think about your friendships, relation-ships, even some of your family members. Are you really happy, or are you convincing yourself that you are? Are they toxic? Is it painful, more so than blissful? Pulling you down more so than inspiring you to move forward?

• Are the people in your life possessive and controlling instead of encouraging you to live authentically and free to be exactly who you are? Think about it for a sec. It's time to wake up and make some real decisions so that we can graduate to the next phase of our lives.

Ask yourself, is this person or this place that you're in worth risking your future? Remember it is you who holds the key. I would ask you to write down names, but I'm not going to because you already know who & what it is. You just have to stop wasting time, be honest and bold enough to do what needs to be done. You've procrastinated long enough. GET TO IT.

EITHER

move forward, or stay stuck where you are. It's your choice.

Chapter Five

THE BRILLIANCE OF TIMEOUT

Like many of you, most of my life I had been constantly and vigorously chasing my dreams instead of living them. I was running myself into the ground day after day, night after night trying to "make it." I never slowed down or was fully present when it came to anything outside of my career. I subconsciously felt if I didn't become a singer, then I had nothing! I wasn't taking care of myself, and I was stressed out in every area of my life, but determined to make it happen and beat the odds that had been stacked up against me.

It was in 2006, a year after giving birth to my son. I began suffering from headaches, ear buzzing, dizziness and equilibrium challenges and I would randomly lose balance or consciousness for moments at a time. I never told anyone because I figured it would just pass eventually.

I was so wrong; it only got worse. By 2009, the Universe had placed me on what I like to call "Time Out," when a routine trip to my gynecologist resulted in an MRI being ordered. The cat scan showed that an AVM (arteriovenous malformation) I was previously diagnosed with had actually doubled in size due to an overwhelming amount of stress and depression. An AVM can develop anywhere in your body but occurs most often in the brain or spine. A brain AVM appears as a tangle of abnormal arteries and veins. I'd say from the photos it looks like a tangled rubber band ball; which can result in significant damage to the brains ability to function properly. That meant; my life was about to take another interesting yet necessary turn.

I suddenly had to have brain surgery, because at any moment I could go into a seizure, have a stroke or suffer an aneurysm. There was also the possibility that I could die; as they needed to pass my heart in order to get to my brain. I had two options.

The first option I was told, was to cut the mass out of my head. But the risks included being permanently weaker on one side of my body, which would include less or no control of my muscle functions even in my face. Resulting in a possible droopy eye or parts of my mouth not being able to move, as well as not having the ability to put things together. But I thought; damn putting things together was my whole life. I create for a living! That's who I am. What would I do if I couldn't create? Something I would only know for sure after the surgery and well into recovery; which would take about four months of down time to heal. I was fine with that But the thought of possibly not being able to put things together; bothered me so much. Especially since I have an aunt who suffered a stroke in her 30's, and I have seen first hand how difficult it is for her to put certain words and things together. So I started researching other alternatives that my doctors hadn't mentioned. I joined an online support group called the 'AVM Survivors Network.' I got to interact with other people going through the same things; and read the stories of some who survived, and some who didn't.

I came across a 2nd option. I could have what's called an embolization and Gamma Knife Radiation. How it works is they would insert a catheter into my femoral artery, and guide it past my heart and up to my brain. Then they pump glue into the affected portion. After it hardens, you then undergo radiation; which hurts like hell because they have to screw a halo literally to your skull while they blast a radiation beam to the affected area. Over time, the mass is supposed to break away into little pieces and be carried out through your blood stream. Sounds simple enough, but this procedure puts you in a hi-risk category for brain

bleeding for two years. So it was pretty much like the phrase 'damned if you do, and damned if you don't.'
I spent a few weeks deciding if I should do it the faster way, and take my chances of possibly losing my ability to create, with possible parts of my face and body not responding when I wanted them to. Or, go with door number two; the long way to recover, and be paranoid for two years while shutting down the grind that I knew as my life.

It's a strange space mentally to be in when you enter the phase of having faith that you're going to live, but preparing to die. I had to start figuring out who would take care of my son if somehow during surgery I didn't wake up. Which in all honesty could happen when folks are meddling inside your head and putting you to sleep with tube down your throat. I had to get my affairs in order and began doing things like my living wills and trusts; it was a lot. But I still never told anyone. I needed a chance to process by myself without all the emotional dramatics and opinions of everyone else. I became extremely quiet and isolated for months. However, I learned something interesting about myself during that time that actually baffled me and still does to this day. I was not afraid to die. I had a very calming peace about it. The only time I became sad was when I thought of leaving my son, because I knew his heart would be broken. But I didn't complain; I wasn't depressed or emotionally distraught, and I never asked why? Maybe it was because I always felt like it was bigger than me, and that I was going through it all for someone else. I was at peace with all of it.

So, I bought two video camera and began filming the entire process. I felt if I didn't make it back; I would be able to show my last day of strength and courage to my son, and that his mommy loved him, and went through it all gracefully. Plus, I made it to where he would have lots of videos to remember me as well as our last moments together. On the flip side; I hoped to educate and inspire someone else with my story. It all sounds so awkward, but I had gotten myself to a place where I was okay. If it was my time, I was ready. I wasn't afraid, and that is something I never thought would be the case when faced with the probability of death.

ON the day of my first surgery; I remember laying on the operating table looking up at all the surgeons and medical staff as the doctors pumped propofol (anesthesia) into my veins. My internal computer began to quickly shut down as all the doctors and nurses began to sound like slow computer-generated voices. When I asked why everyone sounded so strange, the nurse just rubbed my head gently and told me everything was gonna be ok. As I began drifting off; I visualized my little boy, and told him (subconsciously) that I loved him before completely going unconscious.

While under the anesthesia, I remember feeling like I was in a trance, floating in what seemed like a warm, neutral, peaceful place. It looked as if I was floating deep under the ocean but with no water as my body appeared weightless. It felt like a waiting space, so quiet, dark, and extremely calm with only one soft light that was shining on me from a distance as I lay floating in bliss. I really didn't want to leave. I then began hearing my name over and over from what sounded like very far away. I tried to ignore it, because I was in such a peaceful place. But the voice drew closer and closer as I started to focus on it. I guess now when I think back; it was as if I had separated from my body, and I had a choice on whether to come back or not.

When I woke up, the doctors were a bit frazzled as they had been calling my name for quite some time to wake up. When I woke up I remember thinking; "okay, alright, I made it." Although I immediately had a massive migraine. My mother told me one of the first things I said, was "I'm moving to Miami!" I don't know why, nor do I remember saying it because I was in and out of consciousness. I suppose I just had this overwhelming sense that I needed to get to the ocean. That is where I would recover for the next two years.

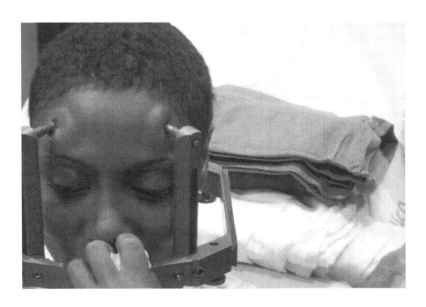

Healing, I knew wasn't going to happen in Los Angeles. So three weeks after the procedure, I packed my bags, left everything I knew, and took my son to the one place I had always found peace – the ocean. Shortly after moving; I learned that I had an extreme spiritual connection to water. It also helped me to heal faster.

ALMOST overnight every-thing changed; as I had no where to go, since right after surgery my brain felt scrambled at even the sound of the wind. I just wanted to stay inside. I had no one to impress. So I took off the fake nails and decided to leave my hair shaved off for a while. I just wanted to get to know myself and my son since I was forced to just be still. I had even got to reintroduce myself to the girl I had left behind; her name is Jesseca.

I had to start learning and compiling a list of all the things that I liked to do, other than my desire to be a singer. I realized I had lost touch with who I was because I honestly didn't know anything other than music. That had been my world, my dream since I was a little girl. But what did I love outside of that? What made me happy other than music? Who am I without all the STUFF? I had absolutely no idea. I found that it was the 'stuff' that made me feel important. But how comfortable was I without it? Without no makeup, hair weave, or fancy clothes, was I even still beautiful to me? Could I just be a mom? Could I feel just as confident, fulfilled and happy just living a 'normal life?' I didn't know what it felt like to just be and I had no idea who I was. But this time I had no choice but to figure it out; because the universe had sat me down, and put me on time out for almost three years.

I began the process of getting to know myself by gathering a list of things that I had never done as well as the things I really enjoyed. For instance; riding in a helicopter, horseback riding, getting a massage, walking on the beach or simply going to the movies. Then I took another step. I started sending out emails asking my closest friend what they thought were my best and worst qualities. It was mind blowing. After that, I started calling and apologizing to people I may have hurt while I was hurting. After all, "hurt people, hurt people." I was just too caught up in my own world to pay attention to the pain I may have brought to others, by being so wrapped up in chasing my dreams and dealing with my own heartache.

One thing I found that I enjoyed; was capturing moments in the form of photographs. So I bought myself a camera and began shooting photos. I also loved to travel and see the world; it made me happy and I had never done it. Shortly after learning to meditate and seeing myself in Egypt in a vision, I felt a strong pulling on my spirit to go there. So I packed my bags, booked a flight and lived amongst the Egyptian locals for almost two weeks. Little did I know that two years later those photos would be in National Geographic and that I would be a noted photographer shooting for celebrities and magazines. It started as just a hobby; something I did that relaxed and inspired me without any pressure.

IF you haven't traveled out of the country, you should. Something in your life shifts when you start to see how people in other countries live. It changes your level of gratitude and ignites an increased level of humility. From that moment on, I started living for me; and not for the amusement or impression of others. I realized that I was good enough just as I was and that was blessed and here for a reason.

Living in Los Angeles, you can get so caught up in competing or keeping up with everyone, while allowing people to chip away little pieces of who you are in order to fit this Hollywood mold. We start changing our faces, bodies and character in an effort to be perfect, accepted, and deemed beautiful. But I've found that perfection doesn't exist. Allowing myself to smile and find the beauty in my flaws - that was beautiful. Being able to laugh instead of picking myself apart was uplifting somehow. It was during my time in Egypt that my spirit began to truly glow. Others even began to notice and say "Hey somethings different about you," or, "wow I didn't realize how beautiful you are." But that only happens when you begin to see the beauty within yourself. It wasn't that I had physically changed. It was simply my spirit was glowing from inner peace.

Chapter Six

ME, MYSELF & HIM

While on Time out, I also got to spend a lot of time hanging out with my son; since Miami was new for us, and we honestly didn't know anyone else. It was just him and I. It's funny, I discovered I actually liked my son a lot. He was so loving with quite a personality. I know, I know, it sounds so bad, but I'm gonna be the mom that's honest and straightforward with you. I never thought that I was built for children, even though surprisingly, they absolutely love me. I didn't know what I was doing when I had a kid; because I never saw myself having any, especially not at the age of 25. I hate to say it, but I didn't truthfully know my son until he was almost four. I loved him more than anything, but did I know him? Not really! I lived on auto-pilot. I never exactly took the time to get to know him consistently. I was so focused on my work and career, as well as trying to balance him, the drama in my life, keep a roof over his head and food on the table. It seemed he was just a responsibility I was stuck with and had to take care of. I was constantly irritated with him. I saw him as needy, nagy, loud, hyperactive, destructive and distracting; especially when I was working. I was also a little bitter after being left as a single mom having to take care of him by myself, with no real help. And that's exactly how I treated him. But I didn't realize it. In my mind, I was doing the best I could to take care of us and work it all out the best way I knew how. But I was barely holding on to my sanity.

But then I stopped and looked at him one day, and I came to the realization that I simply didn't understand his love language, nor did I try to without being frustrated. I also had to check myself because he didn't ask to be here. As much as he got on my nerves, I couldn't see my life without him in it. I never stopped to realize that he loved me more than anybody else on the planet, and that I was his world. I was enough for him. He just wanted to be close to me. He didn't have anyone else.

I sat and thought; Why do I get so agitated and uncomfortable when my son wanted to constantly lay on me or touch me? Why don't I like it? It's just affection? What's the big deal? But then I had an 'Aha moment.' It's because I didn't have that with my parents. It was foreign to me. I don't have any memories of cuddling up under my mom or dad in bed, or them ever rubbing my head or gently touching my face or hugging on me. I didn't even know what that type of affection felt like until I was probably 29.

I remember the man I was dating at the time would gently touch my face as we would talk in bed, and I was like 'ooh that's feels nice.' I'd never felt that sensation, at least not that I could remember. I guess when I was younger; life had gotten incredibly hectic for my family, plus I had two other siblings that needed their attention. There was so much drama between my parents that the showing of gentle affection for me got lost somewhere in the shuffle. So I believe I shut that part of myself off so that I wouldn't need it. Even now, my parents and I show affection very oddly. But, I know they love me, and at the time only doing the best they could.

I spent a great deal of time by myself as a child, and I was quiet with big dreams and extremely introverted. So I had to quickly learn how to open up and give my son something I didn't really have. Once I acknowledged this, I was able to put forth more effort with a better understanding of myself.

I thought about how I treated the men I dated. I had more patience to communicate; I gave them my love, undivided attention and would make time for them whenever they needed me. As I pondered on this, I heard my spirit whisper, "he needs your love just like you would give to a man. Treat him with the same patience, understanding and gentleness." So one day when my son started acting up, I stopped what I was doing and asked him, "What is wrong, why are you acting this way?" I asked without being brash or irritated - but, with love. I asked him to talk to me and that it was ok to express himself and his feelings. Then I said, "If you need some attention, just tell me, and I will stop what I'm doing and give it to you." But you just have to tell me what you need, because I don't know."

From that moment on, when he would come into my room and say, "mommy, I need some attention." I would stop whatever I was doing. I would give him a hug or lay with him, or sit and talk to him about whatever he wanted to share and truly be present. I slow danced with him, looked into his eyes while singing him love songs. Or listen to him tell me stories that he made up, and then after a few minutes he would be over it and off to his room, back to what he was doing and not bother me at all. It was awesome. Now he's older, and will say things like; "mom, can you cuddle with both arms around me? I really like that." He's learned to be very specific about what he needs, that way I don't have to guess. Sometimes I even write him love letters and leave them by his bed so that he can read them when he wakes up. He loves that, and he does the same for me; as we began to learn each other's love language.

Another thing I did was schedule what I called Mommy and Mere Day, a day we go on a date only he and I… no work or computers. Because I can't honestly give him my full attention all the time. So there's a day just for him and I. Instantly; he stopped being so out of control, he began respecting my time and in return I respected his. That's how I began to fully fall in love with my son for the first time. I also began to fall in love with me. I started taking myself out on dates to restaurants, the beach, or on little trips. I took the time to appreciate the beauty in the simplest of things - like a cool breeze, or watching a couple in love smiling at one another. Funny how just being silent and present makes you so aware of what you take for granted.

I also noticed how certain things instantly changed my moods. Like the way a purple orchid makes me smile no matter what's happening. I would fill my house with them and I still do. One year when people asked me what I wanted for my birthday I said, "All I want is for purple orchids to show up all day because they make my heart smile."

Over the course of 2 years I began doing all sorts of things; I didn't wait for anyone else to do them for me. I started taking better care of myself and spent more time in silence; as I meditated every morning on my balcony. I started embracing the fact that this life - without all the other stuff was actually - beautiful. I instantly became inspired and saw that I had much more to give than being a music superstar. There were other things that I could do as I began to look for fulfillment of purpose. I began to ask myself the hard questions. What was I here to do? What is my purpose? Then I would quietly wait for an answer.

Some of you keep going in circles, rushing through life just trying to "make it." Don't wait until life forces you to be put on time out, or you become sick, physically hurt, or in pain before you allow yourself the time to just be in silence. Go away for a few days, take yourself to the beach or the park. But be certain to take that opportunity to evaluate you and what you need. Even if it's just to rest. Put yourself on time out to evaluate where you are, and what's going on around you. That way you never have to be forced to.

SLOW
DOWN
almost everything
can wait!

Chapter Seven

CLIMBING THE MOUNTAIN

AS I prepared to take a two mile or so long walk to a market in Manuel Antonio, Costa Rica, I began dreading the monster steep uphill road. I had endured that road a few days earlier. It depleted me of every single ounce of energy I had; which left me sweaty, irritated with bug bites and sore in places I had never felt before. I contemplated if I should call a taxi to have someone take me there or pay someone to do my grocery shopping for me. Or, if I should just go ahead and do it on my own. It wasn't like I had anywhere else to be. So, I mustered up the energy to do it again. As I was walking, I began to realize that I felt more in control of my breathing. I stopped once to rest for a few seconds, but I was able to pace myself and consistently walk without wobbling like an amateur. My back was straighter. I wasn't huffing and puffing, out of breath or whining to myself. I was able to just enjoy the journey, as I happily said hello to everyone who walked by. I even took pleasure in watching the little monkeys swinging across the phone lines and into the forest.

E ventually, I get to the top of the mountain after an hour long hike, and as I got ready to buy everything I needed, I begin a huge debate with myself. I was contemplating buying a gallon of water vs. getting a smaller bottle of water? Because I thought OMG how am I gonna walk up and down this long mountain carrying all this weight! Should I maybe get a taxi to take me back? Even though they were just personal cars that appeared to be so dangerous and real suspect. I went back and forth in my head thinking; I don't know if I can make it that far with all this stuff. But, I realized if I didn't get the water that day, I was gonna have to go all the way back up the mountain in 2 days to get more. So of course I got everything - because truthfully ain't nobody got time for all that!

I took a breath and began walking up and down the steep one lane road. The weight of everything I was carrying started becoming evident as the handles from the bags began to create marks in my hands and fingers. They began turning bright red from the swelling and lack of circulation to my fingertips. I started encouraging myself by saying things like, "Wow, this is heavy, but it's not that bad, I can make it." I started seeing taxis drive by and slow up next to me. Yet, I decided to let them pass, and instead took small 15 second breaks when needed. I felt strong as I walked. My posture was straight. I felt fit and balanced, my breathing wasn't even scattered or shallow. My body didn't hurt as much and I made it back to my room, inspired, not wore down and exhausted as before. I realized at that moment my body had become conditioned. I was growing stronger with each mountain I faced; because it didn't hurt as much as the first time. I was prepared and knew how to manage it much better the this time around. Such is life.

A lot of times when we have a problem or we're going through something, the first thing we do is look for someone or something to bail us out. What we should do instead, is put on our running shoes and be willing to get sweaty and dirty. We should be have to do the work to condition ourselves for the next level of our lives. Because if we don't, we crumble under the pressure and begin to complain and blame our way through each test; failing miserably. Some of us wonder why the same things keep happening to us over and over. We end up in the same relationships or with a bunch of ex-best friends because they've supposedly all done the same things to us.

I had a friend at one time who had so many 'ex' best friends I had lost count of who she was talking about. She was super needy, selfish and never accountable for the fact that she was actually her own worst enemy. She had ran us all away.

Many of you keep repeating and telling the same pitiful story over and over. Everybody dogs you out, people don't appreciate you, people keep hurting you, nobody believes in you or is trying to help you - blah blah blah. We've heard it all. But the problem is you. You keep repeating the same test because you haven't passed yet. Get it together!

It's time to start climbing your mountains by making a decision to do the work, and take 1 step at a time. Don't try to ignore it or pass it on to someone else to do for you; expecting to be taken to the top, as you just ride. Stop being lazy, prideful, pissed off, bitter, or walking around with a sense of entitlement as if the world owes you something. Because in retrospect, no one owes you anything.

TELL YOURSELF: "I can do this! I am gonna pass this test. I have the courage to do the work to get the results I want. Today, I change my story." It all starts and ends with you. You just have to get over yourself long enough to recognize it.

My journey up the mountain, with all that weight began with me doing one thing - STARTING, and rooting myself on along the way. I didn't know how far I would make it, but I kept going anyway. Now I feel stronger, more confident, clear, focused and very proud of myself for not indulging in the excuses, fears and doubts that often try to creep in to discourage us to give up.

D on't you get tired of constantly waiting for someone else's support or approval before you feel confident enough to make a move? Pay attention, because often times you are setting yourself back months and even years.

Speak up! Be clear, put on your big girl panties or for the fellas, big boy underwear. Stand up for you!!! Go out and get what you want! Stop with the pitiful excuses no one wants to hear, and make it happen. Start the conversations that need to be had. Do the work that needs to be done, so that you can move forward and stop going in circles. Do it. Go now! You don't need anyone else's approval. Stop holding yourself making from making it to the top of the mountain.

Encouragement Affirmation

I will no longer stand in my own way.

I am talented, smart, and the world needs something I have to offer.

I am capable and resourceful.

Abundance follows me where I go.

I will no longer procrastinate and make excuses for why I haven't completed my task or vision.

I will not allow negativity or discouragement to enter into my space or become distracted.

I am blessed, loved and supported.

I am exactly where I'm suppose to be in this moment.

Everything will work itself out.

What is for me, no one can take away.

I haven't missed my opportunities, I'm creating them.

Today I move forward with boldness and passion.

Today will be an amazing, productive and magical day.

Chapter Eight

THE DARK TUNNEL

2012 was one of the hardest years of my life. Most would have never thought that I was homeless living in a motel off Hollywood boulevard called 'The Hollywood Palms Motel' with my seven year old son. All we had was a two-week voucher from the welfare office, food stamps to eat, emergency cash aid for essentials, and absolutely no plan or clue as to what I was going to do. I remember feeling extremely suicidal to the point I eventually checked myself into a mental hospital. I felt so unstable and not myself while being used as target practice for ridicule, death threats, and every other persecutory method the media could conjure up. I had become withdrawn and very silent. I felt completely numb. My hope sputtered in and out like a bad video connection. I just couldn't quite see a clear picture.

I began to question God and I asked; "haven't I been through enough, have I not suffered enough. I mean, what more could you possibly want from me. I'm doing the best I can, why would you allow people to treat me this way all the time? Why do I keep ending up here, How long do I have to suffer, What did I do so wrong? What am I doing wrong? I thought I was in your will, and did everything you've asked me to do so far. I don't understand." I was pissed and so done with it all.

ONE DAY you can feel like you're on your way, moving at a steady pace, walking in the flow of all that had been healed from the past and the next day you're homeless. Not to mention; I had just began to feel proud that I had done the work needed to clear my path and finally, it seemed as if the clouds had begun to shift and the sun was starting to shine on me again. I was able to smile at the fact that I had found peace. True inner peace, and my spirit had found a sense of calm that I had never felt. I was able to proudly lift my head up high without hiding or faking it to mask the pain or the shame that had been placed on me years before. I had a plan on how to set my life in motion. I was excited and filled with anticipation of moving on to the next phase of my journey; especially after having been on spiritual and emotional crutches for so long. I was ready to walk and even sometimes run without limping. I had endured. I even changed my name a few times, and had to change careers which seemed like every year, but I had finally settled and was content on my new path. But what I didn't realize; is that I was being tested on all that I had learned.

One morning after dropping my son off at school I came back to the motel and just felt this overwhelming amount despair, I was emotionally numb and void of feeling walking around as if some sort of zombie, as I looked for work and sent out resumes; my body was shutting down, my skin was pale, dehydrated and lifeless. It never occurred to me I couldn't even cry around that time. I was so weak, and all I could think of was this life was so overrated, and I was tired and over it. I started envisioning ways of how I could end it all. I was tired and I wanted out. Was this really my life? I thought. I didn't deserve to be treated this way. I believed the Universe had turned it's back on me, and there was nothing I could do to please it.

AS I rationally thought of every ridiculous way to end this torture; from walking out into the busy traffic on Sunset Blvd, to driving into a wall, or over a cliff. I ran through every scenario I had access to. But I just couldn't seem to figure out a rational way for my son to understand why I had left him, or how I couldn't break his heart. I had worked so hard to shield his spirit from being broken as a repercussion of my actions or others. In his little world I was all he had, no matter who came and went, it didn't matter to him. I was all he wanted. My son, Chimere didn't care where we lived or what we had, he just wanted to be with his mommy, so for me to hurt him that way; I couldn't rationalize. He was the only thing I could actually feel. I couldn't break my son's heart. Even now, for some reason, it still makes me choke up, as tears try to force their way up from my heart to stream down my face without consent.

So I did what I thought was the most responsible thing to do in situations like that; I reached out for help. I sent a text to 3 of my friends that I knew would be calm, understanding and not send me over the edge, with dumb comments or over-emotional panic. People that I knew had the ability to gently grab me by the shirt, and gradually ease me back from the cliff that my pain had designed. I even called the suicide hot-line, but they made me feel worse as they blatantly treated me like I was a child, so I hung up. There was nothing caring or understanding about it; there was only passive aggressive judgment.

AS I began texting my friends and telling them where I was mentally, they started to find ways to keep me in site or on the phone. My friend DB basically made me ride around with him all day while running errands; as I sat in silence with nothing to say. I just stared out of the window or anything I could find that didn't require me having to look at him; because I knew spiritually he could see into the deepest part of my soul if I did. Even my mom and aunt flew down and stayed in the motel with my son and I just to make sure I was ok, but acted like they were just coming to visit. I knew they were trying to do a subtle intervention.

The people that know me best knew that I would suffer trying to figure it out before I asked them for anything that will cause discomfort or disrupt the flow others. Nor do I like anybody trying to patronize, force me to do anything, or ask entirely too many questions especially when I'm like that. You have to really know how to deal with me, and I have to know that you're sincere, or I become instantly repelled and withdrawn.

Even Jonathan (my spiritual advisor and intuitive life coach) started doing some spiritual reversal work on my behalf. Because I couldn't even so much as pray. He informed me what I was feeling wasn't me, yet it was the energy that many people were directing towards to me.

JUST as a side note. I want to make sure we all understand that when we are saying and thinking negative things about people, in actuality we are sending up negative prayers for them. Keep that in mind next time you start judging and gossiping; even about the people you see on TV or in the media that you don't even know.

I seemed to feel a bit of relief for about 3 days until that heavy dark cloud came over me again and my best friend Janell sent me the address of a mental hospital to check myself into. I knew she was scared, but she was so calm, gentle and understanding. She didn't make me feel judged, even though she literally called and text me every hour. Everyone else for the most part I disappeared from. I didn't want people asking me questions, and I barely took any calls from my family because I felt unstable and confused as to why I couldn't control the thoughts that were in my head. I just had to shut everything out. I had no tears, no emotion, just done with it all. I didn't feel at all like myself and that made me rather nervous; as I randomly switched in and out of this mode I wasn't familiar with.

But then the strangest thing happened. During my psych evaluation, the psychiatrist said, "you're not crazy! You're feeling exactly how anyone else would feel had the same thing happened to them. Your reaction is normal." They offered me medication to take the edge off, but I decided I didn't need it because it wouldn't solve the problem. Plus I'm not the biggest fan of brain altering drugs. But her words in some strange way were comfort enough. I found just merely talking to someone, lifted me quite a bit. I learned if ever you're going through something like that, to where you're so far down you can't climb out, REACH OUT! Let someone know what's going on. You'd be surprised how good it feels to just be heard.

After being released, I remember walking to the car, and everything looked so different from when I went in. The sun was shining so bright, it was such an absolutely beautiful day. As I quieted my mind, I allowed myself to be present in that moment, to the point I could even hear the birds singing in the distance. I began to hear my spirit whisper, "It's ok, you're ok." I took a deep breath and just sat inside the car for a moment in complete silence, not moving. Waiting to hear what my next step would be. Soon enough, things started being revealed to me, and I began to get inspired. I quickly felt my vibration raising, and I immediately went into action with full inspiration. Just 10 months later while writing this chapter, I have my own place, as well as my own 2 story 1600 sq. ft photography studio in North Hollywood that I don't live in or share. I'm shooting covers for magazines of the biggest celebrities and running my own business with all the equipment I could ever dream of, mentoring young adults, producing my owns shows. As well as removing and making peace with the thorns that had been stuck in my side.

I feel strong, I'm inspired, I'm at peace and right now I'm sitting in a beautiful room in Manuel Antonio, Costa Rica deep in the rain forest by myself, over looking the most beautiful ocean, writing the very page you're reading; in hopes to inspire whomever needed to hear this story. For the person who's at their wits end and can see no way out. Just know there's always a way out, you just have to build up the courage to find it. My life changed from struggle and many years of hell. To fulfillment and bliss in a matter of months; right when I thought it my time was up. I just had to stick it out a little while longer. I had no idea my miracle was waiting right around the corner. And to think I was ready to end it all.

Many times these small set backs are just setups to get you to move forward while building your character and the testimony needed to inspire someone else. It all sounds crazy I know? But life can change so fast. Miracles do happen; and they can happen instantly if you change your attitude towards it. Sometimes you have to keep walking through the tunnel; battered and bruised with your bandages and broken heart, towards any little spec of light or the smallest ounce of hope you can find. No matter what it is, just hold on to it. Take your time, and as you continue to move forward that light will slowly began to get bigger and brighter as you near the end of a long hard journey through that temporary tunnel of darkness. Go slow, and simply be willing to listen to what your spirit tells you during the quiet scary moments of uncertainty and pain, when everything is not so clear. The ONLY way to get to the other side is to walk through it. Keep Going!

WHAT

may seem as a set back,
is merely just a set up to
make you uncomfortable
enough to move forward.

Chapter Nine

WAITING YOUR TURN

Years ago, I would get really irritated with the waiting for 'my time' charade. People would always say "your time is coming," or "it's almost your season." I would also hear, as I am sure you have, "This is gonna be your year!" I started getting so sick of hearing what seemed like insincere unwanted babbling. My life was saturated with nothing but more struggle, more hell, more hurt, more drama, more false hopes and more broken dreams to endure, year after year.

While in the midst of those hell-dressed years, you begin to feel like God has forgotten about you while everyone else seems to be getting ahead. The frustrating thing is noticing that some of those getting ahead are significantly less talented than you and don't work as hard. Even worse is being in the company of folks that are always complaining and refusing to see the incredible blessings they have that others are praying for.

At some point, you start to feel like doing the right thing is the wrong way because the people doing all the crazy ridiculous stuff are the ones getting ahead. So as you plow away at what seems like the long hard road, you increasingly become envious of those around you or even the people you see on these reality TV shows. Honestly, it's as if they don't appreciate or deserve to be there. Or how about being around people who appear to have great marriages, and you're still single and looking. You become jealous, sad and pissed off because according to society's standards this is what you should have in order to be complete, or deemed successful.

Have you ever thought that maybe the destination you're looking for is not the final destination at all? Maybe, it's bigger than that as a whole, or possibly what you desire is just a temporary space for learning or acquiring the skills needed for the next phase of your life's journey. Or where you think your life is going; there's the possibility that's not even where you're headed. Have you ever been open to the idea of a different path? Maybe it's bigger and better than the one you see for yourself.

Sometimes the wait forces us to re-examine ourselves because we're missing the bigger picture and often need to be re-routed in an entirely different direction. I've found that one wrong turn can take you out of alignment for years, while you try to recover and heal from the consequences of whatever choice you made.

For instance, I always envisioned myself from a child, being a huge star as a singer and traveling the world with millions of fans; and I was willing to sacrifice everything to get there. I worked so hard at it. But I never in a million years thought I would be a life coach, photographer, talk show host, TV producer or even writing this book right now. But as I began to wait my turn, I started to grow, and purpose started to reveal itself. Things that I once thought were so important, didn't matter as much anymore. I no longer needed the satisfaction and validation that being a super star would give me. I began to crave fulfillment of purpose, healing, and teaching people how to become whole.

Let's skip over to the subject of relationships. Some of us are looking for a companion. But if you had that relationship you so feel you 'need' right now, you couldn't give 100% of your focus to your purpose, inner work, healing from past relationship issues, and other things. Many of you are looking to fill a void that someone else shouldn't be responsible for filling. That is why your man or woman hasn't shown up yet. You haven't done the work needed to keep what you desire once you get it. You will destroy it if you're not ready; or, it will send you so far off your path that it will take you years to get back. Just think about that for a minute. You are exactly where you are supposed to be at this moment. Get to work and submerse yourself in your purpose, and that relationship will organically flow right into your life. And when you're ready for it, and it's your turn next in line; it will take off on a bright sunny day, instead of being forced to see its way through a storm.

Just as a plane slowly backs out and taxis down the runway; moving slowly in line with all the other planes waiting for its turn to take off - so is life! And when you take off, it's fast with a huge amount of momentum as you're thrust into the sky. That's the flight of life. Even then, don't forget that all flights are not direct flights. Sometimes in life you have to come down for a layover. At times even change planes or directions after reaching a particular point or place. You must then rest, refuel and patiently wait for your departure. You can never rush a plane. Everything has to be ready and pass inspection before it can make it safely to your final destination. Not to mention you the pilot, has to complete the training necessary to fly. One negligent move can send you spiraling out of control, and nose-diving to the ground with no real way out. And there are very few that have survived such a crash landing. So in retrospect, the wait is worth your life. You may have to endure a few delays, but at some point you will reach your destination. Although it may not be the most convenient or luxurious way; sometimes you may have to ride coach instead of first class. Or for some; endure the grueling long haul of the bus. Nevertheless; the journey is always necessary for the testimony, but eventually you will still get there. Delays are for a reason.

Many of us think we are so ready for the things we so desire, but in actuality we're not. Some of the places we are headed can destroy us if we're not prepared mentally, physically, and spiritually. For instance; had I made it as a singer years ago, I would probably be somewhere spiritually empty, on drugs with no purpose slowly killing myself with the illusion of what I thought I was suppose to be. I know now I wasn't ready. I wasn't sure of myself; I was easily manipulated and thirsty to make it, which would have made it easy for me to fall into all kinds of stuff. Patience becomes vital. Sometimes we get so frustrated with the wait, not realizing that at this moment, you are exactly where you're suppose to be. When it's your time; nothing can stop it but you.

Now there are other instances when you miss your plane because you weren't ready on time. You were late because you were rushing to get ready. That's okay; it happens to the best of us! But as frustrating as it is - that is the perfect time to stop and say, "Hey, it is what it is, I will be ready next time." Don't beat yourself up. But take the time to really focus and get yourself together. That way, you don't miss your opportunities or have to always get ready, but you stay ready.

Life is full of lessons more so than tragedies. We get so emotionally wound up, caught up in the moment, and detached from the listening to the soft whispers in our spirit that we fail to put ourselves on time out to see what is really going on. We don't take the opportunity to ask, what can I learn from this? So that we can start seeking the lesson and not someone to blame.

The most crucial lessons come through turbulence. Those times in life where you're unexpectedly being tossed from side to side feeling like your world is going to come to an end. Some cry. Some give up. Some begin to pray and call out to God. Or some simply hold on to their seats and tough it out bravely. The outcome lies solely in your thoughts. Thoughts are so powerful. I can't stress enough how what you think about most, is actually what begins to manifest in your life. Your greatest fears become your reality at some point if you continue to dwell on them and send out that energy. We all carry a vibration, and you are responsible for yours - good or bad.

For awhile I was incredibly depressed. I felt as if life had dealt me a bad hand, and no matter how hard I tried to do better there was someone waiting to set me back. That was the story I told myself, and time after time that is exactly what I got. So I came up with something that works amazingly well. I call it my IMC List (Instant Mood Changers). I compiled a list of things that instantly change my mood and energy. I just pick something off my list when I can't seem to lift myself out of a funk, and it works fast. Let's take a moment to compile your list. Remember, you can always add more as you become more aware of the things that make you happy.

My IMC List
(Instant Mood Changers)

Here is a sample of my personal list:

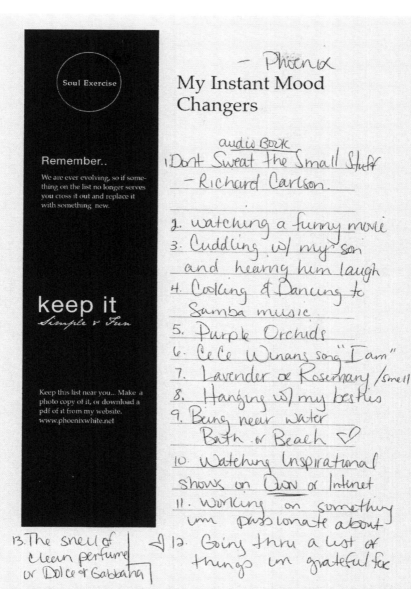

Soul Exercise

Remember..
We are ever evolving, so if something on the list no longer serves you cross it out and replace it with something new.

keep it
Simple & Fun

Keep this list near you... Make a photo copy of it, or download a pdf of it from my website.
www.phoenixwhite.net

— Phoenix

My Instant Mood Changers

audio Book
1. Dont Sweat the Small Stuff
   — Richard Carlson.

2. watching a funny movie
3. Cuddling w/ my son
   and hearing him laugh
4. Cooking & Dancing to
   Samba music.
5. Purple Orchids
6. CeCe Winans song "I am"
7. Lavender or Rosemary /smell
8. Hanging w/ my besties
9. Being near water
   Bath or Beach ♡
10. Watching Inspirational
    shows on Own or Internet
11. Working on something
    im passionate about

13. The smell of
clean perfume
or Dolce & Gabbana

12. Going thru a list of
things im grateful for

Chapter Ten

PRISONER OF TRUTH

This chapter I wrote towards the end of me finalizing this book. I have debated so long on this chapter. But I kept feeling as if I was a prisoner of my truth and a slave to a lie. For years, I've felt like I was backed in and trapped in a corner filled with consistent abuse every time I tried to move forward in my life. I was exhausted with suffering for a crime I didn't commit.

Now, I know that in telling the truth like all things, it comes with consequences. For me, those consequences would come in the form of legal woes if I were to expose certain things. But honestly, none of those concern me because I'm smart enough to know that in the legal world I have nothing to lose, but my sanity when I'm not honest. I'm tired of hiding, and seemingly protecting other people who have only done things for personal gain at the expense of my life. When I decided to write this book, I promised myself that I would be honest, raw and transparent with who I was, and who I am now.

I wrote six pages in explicit detail about what happened that resulted in me being lied on, ridiculed, false accusations of cheating and manipulating a man into believing he had a child that wasn't his then stealing his money, running off with it, never to be heard from again. Not to mention every other scandalous, malicious, evil thing you can think of was said about me; all stemming from a person that I loved with every ounce of me. But no lie, it seemed as if he tried to literally ruin my life, all to save his.

Those pages went something like this:

For the last seven years, I have been held prisoner to my truth. Forced to be silent when all I want is to be free and honest. I'm not angry, but it does still sting a tiny bit when strangers who know nothing about me throw what they've heard in my face as an attempt to bully or belittle me. It always seems to happen at some huge event, red carpet or major moment or opportunity for me. It seems as if I can never get away from it.

I've always been the type of person that's willing to suffer the consequences and karma that come with my actions. But it's unbelievably hard when you have to suffer for a lie in complete silence; hoping that people will grow up. Knowing in my heart no one would really listen, and even if they did, most would only turn the truth into gossip while your honesty is transcribed into you being bitter.

The weight I have had to bear regarding my ex has plagued me in a way I wouldn't wish on my worst enemies, and I have allowed it because of many things. First of course; I just wanted to protect my son. I was and still am constantly being told well if you say something your son is going to suffer for it. Lastly, because I was still protecting the person that was tearing me down in an effort to save themselves. Why because I loved him and didn't want to hurt him. I believed I saw his heart over his actions. Why am I saying something now? Because I'm tired of being held captive and carrying around this heavy weight and I need to set it down. At this point; I'm like F**k it, I choose to be free. When you decide to face things head on instead of always running and hiding from them, they lose their power, and I refuse to be a punching bag any longer.

But; I've decided recently that I'm not going to include those pages that I wrote. Even though, I know that it would be juicy and filled with enough tea to sell a bunch more books and give me an enormous amount of free exposure. And definitely not because I'm afraid and/or under a confidentiality agreement. But because of my integrity to the true purpose of this book and because I'm tired of telling that story of sorrow to myself over and over for the last nine years. I just refuse to be defined by it anymore, or let it control my personal feelings towards my life, my character or my future any longer. Nor, will I hide the truth or shrink in shame from a lie. I will embrace and release all that comes with it.

I am constantly redefining strong as I have learned to turn my pain into purpose and power. But what I will tell you is what I learned from it all, as there is always a lesson in everything. Like any extreme life-altering event in your life, it can either build character, strength, and wisdom; or it can make you weak, fragile and break you down. But it's up to you to choose the effect it will have in your life.

For a while, my pain took me down in every way. But when I actually looked at it, I realized that it has helped me to find out who I really was. It showed me what I was actually capable and made of. I learned how to do things on my own that I always thought I needed other people to do for me. I also learned that no one person is the end of you. I can now relate to so many women and be an example of survival, growth, and forgiveness. I learned that I was more than a relationship. I had a purpose outside of falling in love, and although it's spectacular to be in a beautiful partnership with someone and share your life; when it's over, you can make it without them. Just like you did before.

I remember being so incredibly depressed after my failed relationship. I blamed myself for everything and was angry with my ex for not being and doing all that he had promised us as a family. For not taking care of my heart, and not honoring the sacrifice I made when he pleaded with me to have my child when I was opposed to it. I trusted him, and he had disrespected my trust in every way. From cheating and lying constantly, to giving me an STD, tearing me down and embarrassing me in every way possible. For me, that was enough to start me on the path of pure bitterness. When he left, my world came crashing down. I didn't understand that type of love. He never even came to get his stuff. It was just I can't be faithful, I don't trust myself, I think we should be friends and he was out. But within weeks he immediately had a girlfriend. When I did everything I knew how. I gave my all. Even when he had somehow decided he wanted to take my son and to toss me out like trash. I was stuck thinking what did I do to you? I was confused and completely shattered. I blamed myself for not being enough.

But as I've grown older I realized that my world had already been crashing down way before then. It was me that kept making alterations in my mind to make all the warning signs look like small speed bumps. I was too in love to listen. I felt if I stuck in there with him, it would get better.

But it didn't. I just got more and more tired from running a rat race that never had a finish line.

I have learned the hard way that when a man is not ready there is absolutely nothing you can do about it. Now, like many of you, I've heard all these games and things you supposedly should do to get a man to marry you or commit. Which from what I've often seen ends in divorce later on down the line. Because when a man is not ready, he's just not ready; no matter how much they love you or how great of a person you are.

When my ex began telling me that we should break up because he didn't trust himself, or feel he could be faithful to me. I convinced him to stay by becoming more under-standing of his needs outside of myself. But that's not what I honestly wanted; as it ate away at my self-esteem. It took for him treating me like complete crap, for me to let go. Because I didn't know how to give up on someone, I loved that much. The truth is; in my world I felt like I just wasn't enough. His manager even told me that he would break us up anyhow once he became famous, because I wasn't good enough, and I wasn't beautiful, successful, or hot enough to be seen with. I "was not a good look." I was told that even as recent as last year courtesy of his illustrious pr. team. When honestly it was just being a coward and not being willing to do the right thing in public. Apologies and admission of truth were only spoken behind closed doors.

But back in the day, I didn't know any better. Unconsciously I felt I didn't deserve that type of love, and that I was just being treated badly and abandoned like every other relationship I had ever had. But see, these were actually my personal unconscious thoughts about myself. He didn't make me feel that way. It was my true self-image that was surfacing. I was projecting it on to him and he gave me what I expected. There were things that I thought about myself even before meeting him that I wanted him to validate as not true. To be honest, most of what happened in our relationship I already felt would more than likely happen. It was my fears manifested. Unfortunately; this is the case for many failing relationships.

I recently realized that mine stemmed from abandonment issues as a child, as well as my first love which was from a previous relationship of 5 years. When the man I loved went and got married just two days after trying to be with me and working on what I thought was rekindling our relationship; filled with lots of I love you's, and beautiful kisses. He never told me anything. I only found out because we had a mutual friend.

I remember feeling so used, manipulated, hurt and incredibly naive and stupid. Some how, I quickly buried that pain as if it never existed and ran straight into a new relationship. Maybe I was looking for love, comfort, safety, healing. Honestly I never even thought about it much except for the fact my first love and his new wife were pregnant at the exact same time and months as I was. Our kids are maybe a week apart. Go figure. But I had shut him off from any access to my heart and was numb to very the thought of him.

It wasn't until recently; 11 years later, my first boyfriend and I talked and he all of sudden just started apologizing for every single thing he did, and the different facets of damage & pain he caused in great detail. I just broke down in tears. Who knew! I would of never thought that would have affected me in such a way. But it put a lot of things into perspective as to why my life went into a certain direction. It was also incredibly healing and freeing and I'm so grateful to him for that.

Over time, I've learned what I will not allow in my life, as well as what my weaknesses and strongholds are when it comes to men. I've learned to hold true to what my core values are, and not change on them to satisfy a lack of discipline in someone else or even myself.

There were so many valuable lessons I would not have learned except through 1st hand experience. One of the main things I learned was to take people for their word and not to waiver on mine. I no longer assume what they say is not what they really mean, nor do I create my own interpretation and act accordingly. I learned how not to be a coward; as well as how to spot the coward in someone else.

I also learned how to forgive and be compassionate without being so naive. How to gracefully stand up for myself without letting fear persuade me to back down; as I use to always be so timid. I also learned how to be grateful, to see myself in every situation without placing all the blame on others. I learned that I was much stronger, much wiser, much smarter, and more creative than I could have ever imagined.

Most importantly, I learned how to love and accept myself completely, flaws and all. So I release that story, and I'm grateful for that experience as it made me the phenomenal women I am today who knows her worth and is no longer afraid to have a voice. I wouldn't have had the courage to write this book had I not went through that tumultuous time in my life. So for it all, I am grateful. Not to mention I gave birth to an amazing little person who has also been one of my greatest teachers. He is an example of true love.

Chapter Eleven

FINDING YOUR SANITY

Over time, I've come to realize that many of my problems are not my own. I have allowed many people to come in and disrupt my sanity. Most often, his or her disturbance to my mental clarity and peace would leave me frustrated, irritated with everybody, and extremely unbalanced. I got to the point where I was like, "Oh helllllll no! I'm not doing this anymore!" Many of us are disrupting our own sanity with people we are merely trying to help! People that we aren't even responsible for! Many times; we have friends and family members that just come in taking over. Whether it's with their negative energy, their lack of respect, common courtesy, overwhelming loud personalities or just plain old craziness. Most don't even realize it.

I will be totally honest; there are a few people in my family and even friends that absolutely can not come and stay at my house for longer than a day. They disrupt the entire energy and balance in my home. They're loud, inconsiderate, disrespectful or complain too much. Then there are a few who take on the attitude of entitlement; making others feel like they are obligated to care for and do things for them simply because you're related or a close friend. Does this sound like someone in your family? It may seem harsh, but I had to stop caring about how things seemed because I was losing my sanity simply taking care of others. I won't allow it anymore from anyone, and at this point in my life I honestly don't think twice about it.

I've learned that you have to set the tone and energy for your home and personal space or people will act up, and leave you feeling uncomfortable in your own home or establishment. You are all that you have. If allowed; people will come in and completely perplex your tranquility in every way! So, I've learned just to let people know some things in advance:

• No, you can't come stay with me without a plan anymore. It's super hard trying to have the "what's your plan conversation" with people who have nowhere else to go once they have made it in. I know this oh so well, and it's hell trying to get them out. Especially after they become comfortable with no contribution as if you owe THEM something. Eventually, you have to have the hard talk of "on this date you have to move."

• No, I will not help you continue to wallow under the title of victim because life had to teach you a few lessons in order for you to mature. Or, because you choose to be depressed and lazy with every excuse as to why you can't progress.

• No, you cannot sleep on my couch for a few days or crash for a few weeks with no defined date for your exit anymore. You have no idea how many people have lived with me well over a year with seemingly no intentions of ever leaving! They simply get comfortable with being taken care of.

• No, I won't feel guilty anymore just because I love you, related to you, or possess more than you monetarily and don't want to pay or help with your bills. Nor will I feel obligated to take care of your necessities, especially when you're young and don't even have kids. I no longer feel sorry for you. We all have to figure it out at one point or another.

WHY, you may ask do I feel so strong-ly about these

things? Because me and my big heart have gone broke from a disease I call 'giving out of guilt.' I love to give, but what I've learned is that your blessings get extremely blocked when you give to a person that you don't want to because they made you feel bad in order to get it. Or, when you did something for someone that left you with bills stacked up and leaving you with their debt, but in your name. Some have even stolen your things after you've taken care of them, only to bounce and leave you with the mess they made.

The kicker though, is that most of them don't even care because in their mind you have more than them, so it's ok. I've met some that believe they've done enough to make 'them' feel as if they've contributed; by washing dishes every now and then when asked to do so, or something similar. Yet these same folks complain or are unavailable when you ask them to help with something that matters to you as if it's an inconvenience.

This very ungrateful mentality can leave even the purest of hearts feeling extremely bitter, angry and unappreciated. Which ultimately begins blocking the flow of your blessings. So now, I don't do it unless my spirit truly feels it's right and I feel good about it. You often know the difference when you don't have to think twice about it, or weigh it out. Don't become an enabler of someone's lack of responsibility, laziness, or pride.

IF any of this sounds like things you have allowed or are allowing; it's time to get your sanity back. That includes moving some people off your couch and out of your space so you can regain balance. They'll be all right; a little struggle never hurt nobody. Also, you'd be surprised how fast one can find a job or a place of their own when they feel the pressure to do so. Have a talk out of love, not frustration, and then give them a letter with a move out date and an overview from your discussion.

Make sure you genuinely express that you love them, but its time that you make a few changes in your life. Let them know compassionately but sternly, that you need time to focus on yourself and the family that you are actually responsible for. Not the ones you've taken care of out of guilt and or misguided obligation because of relation or friendship. It's time to move forward.

There are even times when someone calls me to complain (not vent); there is a difference, and I'll explain that later. But, I simply have to say, "can I call you back?" Because at that moment my spirit may be too sensitive to take it in and if I do, it will attach to my energy, and I will start feeling upset and down for no reason. Or, I may have so much of my own stuff going that I can't take on anymore. You have to know your limits and don't feel bad about them.

Now here's a place where I've really struggled. If you're anything like me, I had somehow convinced myself that I was superhuman. I thought I could do everything for everybody, and if I didn't or couldn't, I felt like a failure. If I managed to do it all on a wing and a prayer; I would start to get extremely overwhelmed to where I would shut down for days at a time after completion. I would be unable to do much of anything because I was completely burnt out by the end.

See, I'm a single parent; which means I'm a nanny, the housekeeper, a cook, the driver, the tutor, I do the laundry and the grocery shopping. I am also the CEO of my company; I am highly involved in everything. I'm the decision maker, trainer, photographer, producer, editor, retoucher & creative director. As well as solve any and all problems. I am also the nurturer and the mentor for not just my child, but also other people and the list of responsibilities continue. I try to do it all, at the same time. I for some reason thought that was normal. As if I'm supposed to be able to do all of that with no problem. But I recently found out that's not healthy or as common as I thought. I certainly thought something was wrong with me when I felt defeated. That was until I decided to create some sort of schedule and balance. It was all too much! I was going to have a nervous breakdown.

I will never forget one day I was driving home calmly talking on the phone to a friend of mine, and suddenly my heart started beating really hard and fast unlike I had ever felt before. You could literally see it through my shirt. I didn't know what was happening to me, but it didn't feel normal. I wasn't far from home, but I decided to go ahead and pull over into a Wendy's parking lot. And as soon as I stopped; I suddenly couldn't breathe and was gasping for air. My heart was racing so fast, and I simply couldn't catch my breath. I thought I was having a heart attack or allergic reaction. I tried to calm myself because I knew if I got extremely emotional and irrational,

I would lose complete control as well as the little sips of shallow air I was able to get. So I sat in the front seat of my car frozen, with tears streaming down my face barely breathing; praying in my mind that whatever this was would hopefully pass through me. I was having an anxiety attack. There was no warning, no nothing. I was honestly concerned that I was going to die right there.

I thought I had things under control, but I was actually so stressed out underneath my calm facade that my body shut me all the way down. A few days later, I learned that it's not necessarily a bad thing. Sounds ridiculous I know, but it's your body's natural way of ridding itself of excessive stress. You just have to flow calmly through it as best you can, being as still as possible in order to slow down your heart rate. Cry if you need to, but try to stay as still as possible and focus on one breath at a time, no matter how shallow it feels. Exhale out of your mouth and just focus on your breathing. Very much so like meditating. Trust me it really works.

After recuperating and wrapping my mind around what had just happened; maybe an hour later I felt like a whole new person, so calm and light feeling. It was very strange to say the least. But I felt amazing.

Ok, so back to finding your sanity. One of the things on my list that most moms can relate to is that there is always so much laundry to do. I can't stand it. It's like the never-ending cycle of wash, fold, put away! LOL!

One day I looked around at everything that needed to be done, and was so exhausted, yet I had so many projects to complete for my clients. So, I stopped in mid fold and was like 'I just can't do this right now'. So I jumped on Yelp and Craigslist determined to find someone to clean my house right then. I needed someone immediately, in my area and my budget. Now I know many of you are saying, I can't afford a housekeeper and for some of you that's true. But for others; you are the same person at the nail and hair salon every other week. Or, some of you that never miss that run to Starbucks every morning. I'm just saying, add it up. Another option is to ask for help; simply ask a friend or family member to help you. You never know until you ask.

MY point is; sometimes we must sacrifice your outer vanity, or mild addictions and habit for inner sanity. It doesn't matter what it is. Find a way to make it work for you. Take a moment to figure out how you can relieve yourself from being overwhelmed, and from things toppling over on you. Because if you shut down, everything shuts down - and that is a whole different set of problems that you don't want. So take a break, (yes, you are allowed have one of those) and think about a way you can either eliminate something from your plate or get someone to help you. Don't feel bad about it, because no one that is successful got there by doing everything themselves.

The SECRET

TO SUCCESSFUL PEOPLE IS TO DELEGATE!

There are no rules to life. Find what works for you.

This brings me to my next point. It is imperative to be aware of the times of day in which your spirit is most sensitive and open. Mine is when I first wake up until about 11am. I don't really answer the phone, read certain text messages, talk to clients or talk to anyone (even some family members). Why is this? Because whatever is the first thing I hear or see, sets the tone for my day. Same thing right before I go to sleep. I need silence or soft voices. Even my son knows not to yell, or play with his toys too close to my room early in the morning on the weekends. And he definitely knows not to talk loud directly into my ear

(LOL). It scrambles me. Sounds like a bit much, but that's who I am. Once you truly know yourself, you can communicate that to the people you love and others around you and the more peace you will have. More Peace = Less Stress.

IN the morning give yourself a moment to power up; similar to that of a car. We live in a world fueled by rushing; and the idea that there is never enough time. So we force start ourselves every day; which eventually becomes damaging to the body and our minds operating system. I typically listen to meditation music or something soft. Other times I just lay in the bed in complete silence mentally going over a list of things I'm grateful for, as I visualize what I want the outcome of my day to be like. Then for a few moments, I take cleansing breaths and stretch a bit.

Once I'm up and somewhat grounded I can take on everyone else. But not before! If something even remotely negative steps into my aura field when I first wake up, I'm highly likely to be incredibly moody; as I have to work really hard to shake off the negative energy from someone else's bad day. What many don't understand is that they are unconsciously passing their toxic energy to everyone they encounter!

Now there are some things that can't be changed outwardly, which means you must adjust inwardly; and the way that you are approaching situations. At the end of the day, you are responsible for the energy you put out. So whatever vibration you're sending out, that is what you will get back. If you're constantly irritated with the people in your house, your home will carry that energy. So try coming in smiling, giving hugs and love instead of being pissed off or irritated all the time. Watch how those around you follow suit. They will have no choice. Love is powerful, and everybody wants some of it, whether they realize it or not.

Then there are those that you need to renegotiate with. As we live and continue to grow, we are constantly changing.

So even in our friendships and relationships there may be things that may no longer serve you as you evolve. Be willing to have a talk with your mate or even some friends and renegotiate by communicating what has changed, what you don't like or won't allow because that's not who you are anymore. Or maybe it's something you need more of, that you like or love. For some of you, it could be, as simple as "I'd really love it if you could _____ " instead of assuming they should just know; as your irritation continues to grow and eventually you explode. Which can result in really hurting the people you love.

It's important to start a MORNING RITUAL to get your day going beautifully.
Write down how you can start each day creating balance and then commit to making it your priority; your sanity depends on it.
I've started a list for you to add to. You don't have to use my top 2, but make sure to list things you can commit to daily.

WHAT
you allow, is what will continue.

Soul Exercise

My Morning Ritual

Meditate for 10 mins

Mental list of things I'm grateful for

keep it
Short & Sweet

Soul Exercise

Peace & Balance

List what' is overwhelming you?

What can you do to fix it?

Don't complain about it if you're not willing to make the sacrifice to bring more peace and sanity to yourself!

Chapter Twelve

BALANCE AND BULLSHIT

This chapter I decided to add because I am in the process of recognizing and removing a lot of bullshit. Bullshit that has marked its territory for several years in my life and made itself at home in my space. Some of which I knowingly and unknowingly invited. Now it's time to clean up the mess.

In order to authentically find balance; we must acknowledge, identify and get rid of the bullshit. First things first. You have to look at your life overall and pinpoint the areas that are out of order. You have to be honest. Because what may seem in order; is simply just different masks we use trying to cover up our chaos. Most times we attempt to shield our ego from the harsh reality & acceptance of what may feel like failure, heartaches, disappointment, shame or guilt. There's so much bullshit, which include things & people that we keep around because it's comfortable. It's what we know. But it doesn't feel right. It's stressful, painful, full of sorrow, lack and just downright exhausting as we convince ourselves that it's all good.

Our space is so filled up with bullshit sometimes that we are impaired from thinking straight or clearly enough to figure out what our next move is. We can't even attempt to think we are going to be able to hear God and the whispers from deep within our subconscious. I've found that most of what we hold on to is out of fear. There are a few levels to this. First is the bullshit, underneath that lives ego, and behind the ego is fear. So we need to figure out how to identify and begin to get rid of the fear so that we don't keep making the same mistakes that stop us from moving forward. I for one am tired of being stuck in the bullshit. And since you're reading this book, I'm sure you are too. So let's do some identifying now that we have acknowledged we have a problem.

It is fear that is holding you hostage and your abundance from reaching you. It's not them (whomever they are) stopping you from receiving; it is you. You are the co-creator of your life and your experiences.

Another analogy is like being in an elevator, and it's packed to capacity with all of your fears; blame, bitterness, anger, hopelessness, fraudulent faith and what if's. Every time your elevator door opens, abundance can never get in because it doesn't fit. You are already packed to capacity with bullshit fear. You have no room left to receive. Yet, you are clinging to the very things you need to let go of.

Now let's take that analogy and use it for every part of your life. Starting with the most common stuff. We will never receive the man or woman of our dreams; the career and desires of our heart, or the money that we are capable of receiving until we leap out of fear and become fearless enough to let go of bullshit that I like to call; meantime BS (things that are just temporary.) Your meantime man or woman, your meantime job, sacrificing your meantime health or weight, your meantime situations, all of which we treat and have convinced ourselves will last forever; good or bad. Holding on to bullshit stuff & people until what we want or think is better, comes along. But the truth is, it's not coming because you are already filled to capacity with something else.

So let's start getting rid of some stuff. The best place to start is with your home. You want more, but you don't have the space for more. Some of you can't even slide your hangers one way or another because your closets are stuffed to the limit with bullshit you haven't worn in forever, but you won't let it go. You keep thinking someday, somehow, you're gonna wear it! But here's my take on things. If you can't slide your hangers in your closet to see the next item of clothing, you need to get rid of some stuff. We grow; we change, we evolve. There is no reason you should be trying to force yourself to wear anything in your closet or waiting for the perfect moment that is never going to come. You will never receive more because you don't have the space for anything else. Bag it up!

The next place is your phone book and any other place of personal access. Think about that man or women that you can't wait to get. Do you have any space or time for them? Or is your life so full of random places and things that consume you? Oh and what about that ex or fling you keep running back to every time you get lonely. The one you may have really great sex with or is just a good person that you keep around because it's safe and predictable in the meantime? That my dear; will block you. It's also a spiritual cord that needs to be cut. Otherwise, you have no heart space to attract the person that you desire. Because that space is still occupied by someone else! Release it.

And then there's that old half ass relationship filled with nothing but bullshit. Bullshit that leaves you confused, upset, trying to constantly prove a point in ego driven arguments with someone you know only brings out the worst in you. Or how about the bullshit people that are always the victim yet they continually infect and affect other people's energy by telling them stories about the bullshit situations they allow to consume all of their energy, and a lot of your time; as they constantly need to vent & gossip about it.

L et's also not forget the bullshit people that don't even like you or only there to use you, but you keep them around for entertainment, status or just so you can feel as if you're apart of the IN crowd. Yet they leave you irritable, annoyed and empty every time.

Another example is when you have seemingly good-hearted bullshit people that say they want you, or even love you, but don't want to be with you. Yet will be with someone else. But you always get the bullshit excuse. Even the bullshit job that you can't stand. Or family members who only come around only when they need something. Or how about the bullshit expenses that you're struggling to keep up with but can't afford at the moment. But instead of downsizing, you hold on to it for ego purposes. Why? Why are we keeping all of this bullshit around us! It's taking up too much of our elevator; we have to let some things off.

The truth is, most of the reoccurring bullshit in our lives have stemmed from fear of something, or we wouldn't allow it. Fear of being alone, fear of loss, fear of not being able to do better, fear of never having enough, fear of lack. Fear of failure, fear of looking not as abundant to others. Fear of not being accepted. You get the picture.

ARE you really willing to get rid of some things, even the ones that feel so good temporarily, but leave you feeling awful later? Are you ready to release in order to receive what you want? If so, keep reading...If not, take your time. When you've had enough of the bullshit and you're ready you can always come back.

OK, so by now, you've gotten the point of what I'm trying to relay. It's time to let go. You have been trying to run forward, but get yanked back every time. But it's you that possess the key to unlock the chain, that will allow you to fly.

It's time to stop and take a look at everything. I've even had to ask myself a few times, am I holding on to this for ego because it makes other people feel good about me? Or does this truly make me happy. Do I feel fulfilled and successful to me? Or is this situation making me unhappy? If you're asking these questions, nine times out of ten its because it looks better to others; yet is a burden, negative, hurtful or stressful to you.

You may need to let go of that expensive place, car or even that sexy man or woman you keep running back to and make a few adjustments; without being so concerned about your ego. Many of us are in debt because of ego. We have to let some things go, so we can regain balance and not be so stressed out.

Now there's lots of ways to release spiritual attachments with people but it also requires discipline. You can do this with a guided meditation which is on my affirmation & meditation CD. But another powerful way, is to write the person's name on a piece of paper and burn it. (umm please do this safely in a pot or something away from flammables.) When you're burning it, visualize their face and say I release, and am released from anything and everything that is no longer good for me, I release and am released from_____ and let them go with love.

Do this for as many people as you need that you feel no longer serve you, or only add negativity, sadness, hurt or just needs to go. You can also include family members.

If you are angry or bitter with some of these people, you can write down how you feel or whatever you want to say and haven't said. Take a few deep breaths and burn that too. I'll cover more about this in the next chapter.

But remember after you do this, you have to separate. Most times many people will feel when you have let them go, and you will start getting random phone calls and texts from those you are detaching from. Be gentle, yet honest and careful not to attach yourself or give them emotional access to you. Some you just have to keep it short & simple; others you need to frankly not have any conversation or interaction at all. I call it putting people on #pause. Sounds harsh, but once you get fed up and tired of the bullshit, you'll get the picture.

NOT

everyone you lose is a loss. #LetitGo

Chapter Thirteen

PURGE AND RELEASE

Over the course of a few years (2011 – 2013), I did a lot of clearing work on my heart. It had been broken so many times that I rarely even noticed the fragments of hurt that still lived there. It was only when I had random triggered moments of painful or even beautiful memories that would send me into a downward spiral of emotions, tears, and depression. I didn't realize my ex from several years ago had left an imprint on my soul that I couldn't shake. Until one day, it dawned on me that I hadn't had an actual boyfriend since him; in over seven years.

My life had been torn into fragile little pieces. As I tried to make sense of it all the best way I could. I somehow needed to glue my world back together. It was difficult considering everywhere I went there he was. He was at every store, doctor's office, on every billboard, radio station, and magazine cover. Everywhere I looked I was reminded of him as his fame continued to rise at lightning speed. It was a constant painful reminder of what once was, causing a massive amount of hurt and torture that was hard to ignore. I couldn't seem to get away from him. But that wasn't all, I was always being attacked, scrutinized, and sabotaged by people who didn't know me. My story or ours.

I lost my record deal, work contracts, as well as many business and personal relationships; some before they even got off the launching pad. People seemed to judge me with the highest and harshest sentiment. But no one ever asked me anything. Except to tell them things to bash my ex, which is not hard, especially when you're hurt. But I refused and silently took the beatings to my character, my work, my dreams, and my spirit for over seven years. You have no idea how hard it is to hold your head up in a room full of people looking down on you, as you try to gracefully smile and say nothing.

As I began to do healing, forgiveness and love meditations to start clearing out my emotional attachments; an opportunity arose as my ex, and I were forced to speak face to face. We exchanged numbers, and I asked him if we could spend some time together so that we could begin to heal. I needed that, and so did he. I had so many things I needed to get out, so that I could release myself somehow and move on. There was so much I didn't understand. It was like something was stuck inside of my spirit holding my heart hostage and I had not been unable to break free. Seven years later, and I was still affected by something as small as a photo. Why? That didn't happen with any other person I had been with.

I realized the reason was that I still loved him. I was not

in love anymore, and had no true desire to be with him, but he had a place that had been embedded in my heart. There was a chapter we never closed, we just ignored it. It was like a never-ending journey of a beautiful love story gone rogue, and I had locked it away in my inner box of keepsakes. I was plagued with memories of him. It was no small thing. This man was someone I would have died for. We had planned to marry and spend the rest of our lives with together. I didn't fall in love with the persona he portrayed; that didn't exist when I met him, but the man inside that few rarely got to see. He was special, genuine, humble, loving, and he was my best friend. I believed had it not been for fame; we would probably still be together. Or. it could have been a beautiful well played lie, and I fell for it.

 angry as I was prepared to be during our meeting after years of fighting about what he calls a big misunderstand-

ing; (in which I will simply agree to disagree) we were finally placed alone in a room. For several moments, we just stared at each other. I didn't recognize the person looking back at me initially. I didn't feel safe with this "stranger" that had an amazing resemblance to the man I once knew.

All of sudden he said something that he and I both knew was bogus bullshit; and we both exploded, going clean off on each other for a few minutes. Because this time I wasn't having it. But then we caught ourselves, apologized for yelling, took a breath and paused for a moment. Our high powered lawyers anxiously listened outside the door, something they admittedly had never done before. But we needed to do this on our own, with no outside interaction.

Eventually, he let his guard down and allowed me to see him, and I melted as I stared into his eyes, recognizing the man I use to know. I just wanted to cry and hug him, for no reason other than I missed him so much - the real him. I completely stopped thinking about why we were there. I even asked him for a hug, because to be honest; we both needed it in order to actually move forward.

After telling him some of the things that had happened as a result of "our misunderstanding", I began to have compassion for him as he quietly allowed himself to openly listen to me, and give me the opportunity to say what was on my heart. I believe he did so because I too let my guard down, baring my soul and the transparent wounds I had accumulated. I didn't try to be tough, or emotionless, nor was I over emotional either. I wasn't trying to make him feel any particular way; good or bad. I just wanted my truth to be heard.

We were finally able to express ourselves without anger. Allowing our walls to come down to be vulnerable and completely honest without fear, since we both agreed we needed to heal. There were so many things that had happened that either one of us didn't know about because we hadn't communicated in years. But the revelation of those things instantly replaced bitterness with an immense amount of compassion and forgiveness.

WE went back and forth for a total of 16 hours straight. There were even moments when I cried, and I don't like to cry in front of others much. We also laughed at some of the incredible moments we shared in the past. I allowed myself to be free regardless of how weak it may have come across. Because to me it was a reflection of strength. This process resulted in a massive amount of release for me. I got to express my heart, my truth, my hurt, my struggle, my pain and my sacrifice. But I did it gracefully. And so did he. I could then let go.

Now, I'm not saying that everything was healed and fixed or that anything drastically or permanently changed in our relationship or dynamic. Because people can be open one day and revert to their old ways two seconds later. But what I am grateful for, is that I got a chance to purge and get it out. It did something for me. It released a lock on my heart that was blocking me from attracting and actually accepting romantic love from anyone. Of course, I didn't realize I had unconsciously done this as a sort of protection mechanism. But I knew I was completely blocked.

ONE day I had an 'Aha' moment, I realized that I have an overwhelming passion for giving love, and I did so freely and openly. I was constantly attracting and falling for men that were emotionally or romantically unavailable to give unrestricted love. Yet, I found myself showering them with it; trying to help heal what someone else had broken. Not realizing the people we attract are mirrors of ourselves in one way or another. I was unconsciously trying to heal them in the same ways I needed to be healed. I had somehow stopped trusting a man's perception of what love was. It seemed everyone that was supposed to love me, hurt me in ways I thought weren't the ordinary couple fights. They went into massive demolition mode, or just abandoned me. For the last few years, I seemed to have dated guys that no longer trusted love; while I did everything I could to show them what it was suppose to genuinely look like. I was determined not to give up on them. No matter what they did to push me away. Because that's essentially what I wanted. Someone to love me enough to fight for me.

So in essence, I began unconsciously hurting myself over and over again. Trying to be loved by someone who was incapable of giving it to me, yet remaining loyal to them. But I really wanted someone to help ME heal. Someone who took the time to love me in MY love language, someone that adored me just as I was. Someone who made me feel as if I was enough for them. But only I could break that cycle. I needed to find those things in myself first before anyone else could.

I've found in life, most of us just want to be heard and

seen. That's why social media is so HUGE. It gives people an outlet to express themselves on a global scale. While judging our worth by likes and followers that make us feel admired, accepted, or rejected.

Back to the story. That day, my ex thanked me for forgiving him. I also asked for the same forgiveness in any area he may have felt I hurt him. Although there is still more healing to be done; I can tell you there is so much weight that can be lifted off of you from just one conversation of pure grown up communication. And doing so, without pointing fingers or looking to place blame – but merely looking through the windows of compassion is key.

The point of this story is that many of us can't get past the anger, regret, disappointment, and bitterness that we're harvesting in our souls. We're stuck because we're not willing to have an honest, compassionate and vulnerable conversation without the over-emotional extra stuff due to the broken promise. We need to get to the core of our pain and express it with love and compassion.

NOW,

I'm not going to lie and tell you it's easy, or you won't have moments where you burst into a volcano of erupting emotions. But being willing to see yourself in the person that hurt you is imperative. Also, listening to a person's spirit by being present and selfless takes courage. That's real strength.

It's easy to yell, scream, point the finger and play the blame game. But to do the work to sort through a problem with a calm and compassionate spirit; well that is to be commended, even to receive it takes an immense amount of love and courage.

Communication with Love is Key

Think of one person that you need to close a chapter with that's holding your heart or emotions hostage! Be honest with yourself, you're the only one holding you back. You have to decide if holding on to your pain is worth the price of your future. If you don't release it, you will never be able to truly move forward.

Next I want you to ask if they would 'allow' you to be honest, and have a real grown up conversation. Let them know that you are asking for an opportunity to share some things on your heart, as you are doing some inner work and healing. And, in return you would also be quiet and provide them the opportunity to do the same. Let them know the idea is to do this with; no yelling, no blaming, no dramatic emotions or loud talking, but a real respectful grown up conversation.

Don't be surprised if you find that some people are not ready to do that or mature enough to handle it, and that's ok. Don't push it. Just sit down and write a letter to them. Not an angry pissed off letter, but one that is vulnerable, clear, and honest. Be willing to also look at yourself to see if you were the cause of some part of it. (Nine times out of ten you were!) What could you have done differently?

The object of this exercise is to purge your heart of as much trapped pain as possible. This is a way of releasing.
Now here's a more intense version. If you're ready for that; Keep reading!

ONE day, I was honored to meet a very old and wise spirit, who didn't know me at all. She came to me and said, "You have so much hurt trapped in here," as she pointed to my heart.

"Once you get all of this stuff out, you will be able to fly like the Phoenix." As she chuckled, knowing that was my name. "Here is what I want you to do. I need you to scream as loud as you can and curse, really go off, you have to get it out" she said. I looked at her like she was kidding, but she was very serious. I had never actually screamed or cursed irrationally at the wind or just because. I guess I'm a bit chill in this way (but I have gone off via text a time or two) otherwise, I just suppressed and kept it all inside.

NEXT she said, "I need to you to write down all of the things that hurt you and go off as if you're talking to those people as you're writing." I was like that's easy; it's the people who owe me money LOL (considering the fact I had financial issues at the time). But boy was I wrong! I went home, grabbed a stack of printer paper and started writing. About an hour later I had written over 100 pages filled with pain and anger. I was in awe as I gazed at the floor at all the papers I had thrown as I completed them. I then gathered them up for the next thing she told me to do - set them on fire and spread the ashes over a river. I had what seemed like a burial ceremony for my pain. I was laying them to rest. I'm telling you; I wrote down things all the way from when I was a child on up.

The scariest part I think was the screaming at the top of my lungs. I thought, "where in the hell am I gonna do that at?" So I got in the car in the middle of the night and started driving down a long road and decided that I would do it there. When I screamed; it was as if something awakened in the deepest part of my soul, and a huge wave of chills ran up the back of my spine like a snake and scared the hell out of me. The energy in my car was so intense and thick that I had to literally roll the windows down to let it out in freezing cold 30-degree weather. I was like WHOA! What was that! I swear I had spiritually unlocked Pandora's box, and a flood came rushing through me.

Here's a picture from that day and my process. It still baffles me every time I look at it, and being able to physically see how much pain I was carrying around with me. But this is an excellent way to purge. I then released it by setting them on fire and hiking to a lake where I spent some time with God and spread the ashes over the water with the intent of letting them go; while I watched them float away.

Literally over
100 pages

Actual Picture

The amount of pain that
was trapped in me.

Chapter Fourteen

THE APOLOGY

I heard Iyanla Vanzant say one day, "Long exten-sions of pain render you unconscious." Many of us don't realize that we spend so much time embed-ding our recycled stories of pain, heartache, and disappointment into our DNA. There are secretly so many things that we are ashamed of eating away at us, and we don't even know it. I'm talking about those deeply buried parts where we had fallen short in the past that we act as if never existed. People that we have hurt, scarred or even broken.

SO many of us are guilty of not protecting ourselves and ending up in situations where we only blame others for the damage caused, when we are also part the blame with our bad decisions and lack of courage to say no. But we don't want to own up to it. Here's an example of what I mean. In my case, I held on to the story of being so played by my son's biological father. As well as, the harsh fact that I simply don't like him as a person because of the way that he's treated our son due to his personal problems, insecurities and feelings of victimization by others. When he is the cause of his own issues as a result of his actions.

I'm not a fan of his, and I'm ok with that, because he contributes nothing to our child and never shows up. Our son and I lived maybe 3 minutes away, and we still haven't seen or heard from him for more than a year now. Why? Because he has an attitude with me for asking him to be accountable for what he says and does. I didn't want our son to get use to always being disappointed and feeling as if he wasn't enough for his father; as he constantly breaks his promises and leaves our son waiting for him to show up without even a courtesy call or hello on birthdays and holidays unless I prompt him to do so. This is also the same person who drives around everyday in a custom Lamborghini yet told us he couldn't help, not even with groceries because he was broke.

Not to mention; I have very low toleration for disrespectful people who believe they can touch and grope on you whenever they want, even in public, with the immature excuse of, "I can't help it" and have nothing more to talk about other than themselves; their success, and constant gestures of wanting sex. He would even at one time come over to my house when he was suppose to be spending time with our son and get in my bed while I worked in my living room and refused to get out of it, no matter how many times I asked him to please come out. Just blatantly disrespectful. As I really tried to be nice, so that he would stick around for our child. I would often wonder and even asked if there was anything else to him. It sucks because he's so brilliant when it comes to his gift of music. But outside of that. There was nothing but a shallow shell of a man with power and status. Needless to say, I did my absolute best for at least a year to be silent, tolerate the disrespect, fondling, lies and charming offers to help, only for him to back out every time or treat me like a begging peasant for something he offered.

But the straw that broke the camels back was when he told me I was a bad parent, and that it was my fault when our son was acting up in school for a brief period. Or when I had to send him away for a year to live with my relatives while I got myself back on track. He threw it in my face, and I snapped. Because it was the hardest, selfless, decision I ever had to make as a single parent. Not to mention he says to me, let's send our son to live with his parents in Oklahoma! When we don't know them or even had so much as been introduced. He doesn't even know his father much. Why on earth would I do that to my baby when both of his parents live 4 blocks from each other. But yet his fathers solution was to send him away so that he wouldn't have to give any money to me. Yet says, as if it was a convincing bonus, "I mean, I'm gonna have to pay a lot of money to put our son in private school, because my parents wouldn't allow him to go to public school. They would only allow the best education for him."

I was baffled and instantly perturbed because I didn't understand why he couldn't do that while our son lived 3 minutes from him. What he was basically saying, was that magically funds would just appear if he was in his parent's care, while I'm here being patient and understanding of this supposed "hard time" he was having financially. Just trifling. It was an insult to my intelligence. Not to mention a slew of other crazy stuff that I will keep to myself for his sake. I was done. But I did try. I really did. He just didn't care unless it was to his benefit, even when I convinced myself at one time he was different and was doing his best. Because for a good month or two. We had made much progress, or at least I thought. As I called myself tolerating certain things that just progressively got worse. But at least we were cordial. No matter what I did, how often I swallowed my pride and kept my mouth shut, or did my best to create a peaceful family unit. It didn't matter.

TO any woman or man going through something similar, and allowing someone to constantly disrespect you for the sake of your child. Stop it! You do not have to tolerate manipulation or sexual harassment just to get someone to co-parent. My father always taught me, if a man or woman wants to be in a child's life, they will be. It's time out for all the other abusive bullshit that we convince ourselves is doing it for the kids. Because the same kids that you call yourself looking out for, are the sames ones that are watching you. They see, feel, and comprehend a whole lot more than you think. Set some ground rules and stop allowing the disrespectful bullshit. It's not ok, its manipulation.

BUT

here's where I get real with my stuff.. When I say it took a whole lot to get me to this point. I mean this took a real take a deep breath moment to admit outside of me being the victim.

But what the f**k was I thinking when I had unprotected sex with a man that I already knew wasn't a good person to begin with. A man that I was repelled by the moment we met. He was rude and belittling to me the first day I met him. A man that I knew had issues! That I knew had multiple women and kids. Why didn't I protect MYSELF from him? Yes, I knew he was powerful and could ruin my career, make me look stupid and all the other fears that I mentioned in previous chapters as to why I did it and blah blah blah. But what was I really expecting to get from him? He didn't like me. I knew he was perverted and charming. I knew he was only acting interested 1 night to get me comfortable enough to have sex with him. But what did I really think would happen? I ignored every single warning sign.

Now, during the process, he made me feel like I mattered to him, he even cuddled with me for hours laughing and talking. Honestly the whole experience at the moment made me feel like I was making love to my man. But I wasn't. That harsh reality came when I got a tap on my shoulder early in the morning at 6 am telling me I had to go. No breakfast, no kiss, no smiling face. Just a simple bye and a door slam. I remember the embarrassment I felt. The shame ate ferociously at me as I rolled away feeling stupid, empty, naive, played. I was so ashamed of myself. All to feel special & wanted by someone that I thought was important. I had convinced myself, wow he wanted me. He had been patient and had given me his full attention, as I shared my dreams and ideas. He waited patiently plotting; until I felt comfortable enough to give in to watching TV in his room. Only for me to leave feeling so empty. I remember erasing his number as I drove the long way home to my then close friend's house that I was with everyday, whom I told everything to and felt safe with. He was the only one I could confide in that I didn't feel would judge me. I felt like trash on the sidewalk that someone had tossed out of a window. Used and no longer needed.

Although my close friend and I swore we would never became intimate, we did a couple weeks after. Six weeks later, I found out I was pregnant during a random STD test after he told me he was having his annual UTI (urinary tract infection.) But I knew better because that is extremely rare in men, so I told him to get tested. My close friend and I had somehow still fallen in love during the course of that month; even though he had given me an std. What was I thinking you ask? I just wanted to be wanted. I wanted to be loved. I wanted to matter to someone, anyone. Plus, I knew he didn't do it on purpose, so I instantly forgave him. But in essence I was broken; so I filled my brokenness with more pain and unconscious chaos.

H owever, now I was pregnant, confused, had a secret boyfriend, secret pregnancy, scared and just went along with whatever came. I was completely out of alignment, ignoring every caution sign I was given. See, I had a habit of convincing myself that everything was ok, and I was living a fairytale. When it was all really a nightmare filled with bad decisions and consequences.

Although my intentions were pure, and I thought I had done the right thing by listening to outside counsel. I was living a lie because I didn't want to let go of the dysfunctional fairytale I had created to make my shame feel better. So my child was born into chaos. I have always felt guilty about that. Guilty that he doesn't have a biological father in his life. Which granted I tried to fix, but I couldn't allow his disrespect in general for women, lack of concern, help or support for our child. But nevertheless, I still felt bad, that he doesn't have a biological father around.

I felt guilty and ashamed for having sex with two men weeks apart without protecting myself. I still felt guilty for not being what I believed a great mom was while working so hard trying to be super human and falling short as I tried to get my career going when he was younger. There were so many skeletons in my closet that were weighing me down.

But one day, I decided to apologize and make everything right the best way I knew how. I apologized to my son's father for not telling him our son was his 'for sure' until he was one years old. Even though I was honest and told him of the possibility when I was pregnant; it didn't matter. I knew for him he needed that apology and despite my feelings about his overall character; I knew he needed that.

So I pushed my pride to the side, looked him in the eyes and apologized with heartfelt sincerity.

I also apologized to my ex love for whatever I may have done that caused our fighting. Because honestly we were both so young and didn't know any better and we drug one another through hell. So I'm sure he hurt as much as I did.

I then apologized to my son, for putting him in this situation to begin with. For all the unanswered questions, hidden hurt, as well as for him not having his father around. I held myself accountable for that void in his life. Regardless of the reason.

Lastly, I apologized and forgave myself for not taking care of me. For putting myself in these chaotic situations. For giving my body, trust and heart to people that barely even liked me. I forgave myself for looking the other way and not having the courage to say no. I forgave myself for not being completely honest with my tainted reflection that was staring back at me. I owned my mistakes and stopped hiding behind the victimization of it all; took a breath and moved forward with grace and release.

No longer am I walking around with my head hung low, wondering if people know my secret or if they are judging me from afar. I'm no longer beating myself up from something that happened years ago. No more hiding. No more faking.

And you know what? The moment I forgave myself, it was as if this heavy chain that had attached itself to my soul that would only allow me to go so far before it stopped me or things fell apart. It just simply detached, and my life completely took off.

L et me ask you something. What is it that you're hiding from in your past that you are too ashamed to admit? Who do you know that needs an apology no matter how much you can't stand them or feel they were in the wrong. Most times there's always some part in there that we attributed to, that was a result of our own pain.

Here's a simple way to forgive yourself. If you don't know how: Find a quiet sacred space. I tend to do this in the bath with candles and soft music. Or anywhere you feel at peace. I then place my hand over my heart and start to pull up those images in my mind that I'm ashamed of or feel guilty about. And as they come up I began to say inward or out loud; "I forgive you." Now don't be surprised if you get angry or start to cry or even attempt to rationalize it. That's all normal. There's no wrong way to do it. But you have to FEEL it, and allow your body to purge however it needs to. Just go with it.

Then began replacing your thoughts with positive affirmations.

While doing this meditation, I begin to visualize my heart with a bunch of band-aids on it as I peel them off. Mine looks more like a diamond heart in a glass case. But yours will probably look like something different, so just go with it. I then start filling all the cracked places with a bright white light as it starts to working as a surgeon to repair the damage.

This may sound insane, but trust me when I say it really works.

Another meditation that I have used that works incredibly well, is by visualizing myself walking or flying up to the top of super high grassy green mountain. Everyone's may be different. I often start coughing in real life during meditation as it gets harder to breathe for me at times as I go higher up to get to the top. (This is a result of my vibration rising.) Once at the peak, God is there waiting for me. There are angels all around in the sky in a huge circular type barricade (yours may differ.) Then one by one the angels bring people up the mountain as I notice their energy, expression, the way they feel (this is where I see who they really are, or what they honestly think of themselves. It's astounding how the true reflection of these people appear as they come up the mountain.

We then face one another, as I place my left hand on their heart and they do the same to mine. It looks like a circular exchange of energy. In essence, you are speaking directly to that persons spirit) its absolutely fascinating. I then say "I forgive you." But I do it with an immense amount of compassion and love. Sometimes God even steps in and talks to them. It varies by person. But that's a method I have found that helps me tremendously.

Keep in mind these are not religious driven exercises, These are ways to connect spiritually. You can adjust wherever your spirit feels necessary. As long as you keep the intention on forgiveness.

LIFE
is too short to be waiting
for somebody to act right.

SELF-FORGIVENESS
Affirmations

- Today I release and no longer carry the heavy weight of shame, guilt, embarrassment and doubt.

- Today I release and am released from the mistakes in my past, and I walk boldly into my future.

- Today I forgive all of me for the hurt and pain I may have caused others and myself.

- Today I release and am released from rage and anger as I set my past free and I forgive myself for my participation.

- Today I release the story that I have been telling myself that has caused me to stay stuck, and I allow myself to move forward.

Self-Forgiveness Affirmations

- Today I release and am released from all forms of self-sabotage in my future and I cancel out anything that was said or done in my past.

- Today I accept and embrace my past as it has helped me to become the amazing person I am today as I grow more patient, compassionate and understanding of others by forgiving myself.

- Today I walk proudly into my future and release all doubts and fear I'm afraid will hold me back.

- Today I release and am released from anything that no longer serves my higher good.

- Today I release anything that blocks me from receiving and giving love.

- I deserve love, I deserve forgiveness. I am love; I am light, and I give myself permission to surrender and let go.

THERE

is beauty in your flaws
and power in your pain.
Embrace it, and use it to
blossom.

— Phoenix White

Chapter Fifteen

GETTING YOUR SWAG BACK

Ladies this chapter is just for you. Can we admit, sister-to-sister, that over the course of time; our life & experiences begin to weigh on the essence of our spirit. For some of us, we become comfortable and complacent feeling stuck where we are? We begin to immerse ourselves in the rush of what feels like a universal shortening of time leaving us with not enough hours in a day to complete our never-ending task list. We struggle to balance the needs of our families, and the demand of our home, work, and school schedules. With all of that going on, the last thing we have time to think about is what we look like or how

'WE' feel. At some point, we start looking in the mirror and mumbling things under our breath like; "Whatever, I don't have time" or 'This is as good as it's gonna get." Or perhaps it's "If only I could afford better or had access to a better this or that." The list of woes and excuses goes on and on.

LADIES if this sounds like you; you have become desensitized, while walking around looking like life has beaten you down, and you don't even realize it. Yet you're repeatedly claiming that you want or deserve better. There are even some of you that are married and barely even have sex or hang out with your spouse anymore. No dates, quality time or special moments. Some of you can barely even remember the last time you dressed up for your man or even attempted to put on something sexy for bed. You're just operating on auto-pilot acting like roommates. Many of you don't feel sexy or confident anymore because you have gotten comfortable in your position and no longer feel the need to impress your man because you've caught him now. Or, you've allowed your body or self-image to get out of hand with a boat load of excuses. Many of you are even unconsciously using razor sharp words that cut into the core of your confidence because you lack the discipline & courage to change it. But if you really think about it, that's most men's fear.

I personally don't get it, and quite frankly it bothers me quite a bit. So were you just treating yourself well because you wanted to catch a man, then start looking a hot mess and he's just supposed to get over it because he loves you? No ma'am. You need to get it together. Not just for him, but for you! Aren't you tired of making excuses for and to yourself? Do something about it! Stop being lazy, care a bit more.

It's time to get your swag back and change the story you keep telling yourself so that you can begin to feel good about YOU again. Yes, it's hard, but so what! Get to walking around your block or something, nobody wants to hear your excuses anymore, or dwell in the presence of your lack of care. Do something about it. You are only cheating yourself out of your best life if you don't.

FELLAS if you're reading this and you are with a woman who has lost her swag or vice versa. Take the time to hold each other accountable. Start taking walks and working out together. Be proactive as a team. Eat better as a family. Inspire and encourage one another to do better. Because it goes both ways. You want your mate to feel at their best. Sometimes they just need a little boost.

There is also the handful of us whose confidence is so shaky, that even when someone even gives you the slightest compliment you throw it back at them by pointing out how much of a mess you look, or how the outfit you were complimented on was so old and so on. Yep, I've been there before and didn't even realize it; as I was consistently downplaying and dissing myself. I, like many;

was never really present or listening to anyone. I would unconsciously blurt out something from my catalog of default responses. That was until one day, it was brought to my attention. I was quickly checked and told to just smile and allow myself to actually take IN the compliment, instead of pointing out all of my so called flaws. Or, letting it go in one ear, and out the other. But to give it it's own moment. Allow yourself to FEEL it! Then just simply say 'thank you.'

What many of us don't discern, is that those random times at the market, when you just run out real quick with no makeup, and don't want to be seen or bothered. (Which so happens to be the time when you randomly get approached the most with compliments) It's really the ointment for some of your wounds. To hear someone genuinely say "wow, I just wanted you to know that you are so beautiful!" That's a gift. It's uplifting and healing your spirit whether you know it or not. But we've been conditioned to brush it off as an annoyance, or something that couldn't quite possibly be true because you weren't all decked out. We need to allow ourselves to take it in and genuinely appreciate the gift instead of throwing it back unopened.

The one thing I have discovered is that people often treat me the exact way that I treat and see myself. What I honestly believe deep down in my soul is exactly what I attract. Some may argue this point, but it's true, and no matter how much I may not want to accept it. The people I often encounter are mirrors of myself in some aspect one way or another. You attract the story that you keep telling yourself.

Here's a good example: In my 20's I thought I was only cute when I wore a wig or super-long weave, a bunch of makeup, some cute clothes and viola! I had transformed into a star just as confident as I could be, or so I thought. I would spend so much time in the mirror perfecting myself trying to mimic the airbrushed girls in the magazines. It never occurred to me that they looked nothing like that in real life. I was constantly looking at myself to make sure everything was so-called perfect. I wanted to be beautiful to the very men I would notice were only interested in what I was showing. I would get so irritated that these men never wanted to just talk or get to know me. They only thing they wanted from me was sex. Why was that? Because, I attracted it!

I spent so much time focused on the outside, while ignoring my own brilliance, intelligence and talent on the inside that no one saw much of. I only showed them my vanity, and vanity is what I got in return; which led to a lot of pain. I wasn't my authentic self. To be honest; I'm not sure I even knew what that was. Maybe in some strange way I thought that being smart wasn't good enough. I was often told in this industry of entertainment that I knew too much, and I would never get ahead if I didn't dumb down a bit. Sounds ridiculous I know, but that is what I was told when I first moved to Los Angeles. The way I looked took precedent over my talent, and I naively went with the flow.

Eventually, I began to feel empty and used by many. Plus, I was out in LA on my own trying to so-called 'make it'. I found myself sleeping in my car and moving from couch to couch, hoping to get an opportunity. But I found myself the prey of many hidden agendas in the form of gracious hosts, that I had to always fight off, or give in to at night. Not realizing that my confidence was being chipped away with every naive or bad decision I had made searching for love from a man.

By the time I hit 26 I was spiritually a hot mess. I hid it well on the outside, but I cried a lot from heartbreak on the inside. I felt like my dreams were over since I now found myself a single mother with no plan. Constantly wondering, how did I get here? I still put on my pretty little mask every day, but on the inside I felt like I was living in a concrete shelter. I was pissed off with no real hope; as I continued to bleed through my band-aid of vanity while attempting to cover up and nurse my wounds the best way I knew how. Essentially, people were repelled by my energy and my lack of care for much of anything, except for my neediness to be loved and accepted by someone, anyone. My attitude became cold and stank as everyone and everything around me appeared to be out to sabotage or hurt me in the most catastrophic ways on purpose. It seemed they all wanted something from me - so I thought. I like many of you; was drowning in a pool of broken dreams and promises I had made to myself.

I wanted more for me. But I couldn't figure out where I was going wrong, until I ended up in Miami recuperating from brain surgery. I began to see everything differently. I started to focus on taking care of me. I began with asking myself the hard questions and accepting the truth of what I had become. I began searching for something deeper. Eventually; I asked "what am I here for? What is my purpose? Who I am, Really?" Finally, the light bulb went off, and I got it. I really got it!

Let me warn you though! Self-realization doesn't always feel good in the beginning. It can have you feeling disgusted with who you are, ashamed, hurt, irritated, angry, emotional, ego bruised you name it. I realized I was operating on seriously fraudulent confidence. We've all heard the phrase, "fake it till you make it." Well, I was over it and done with faking it. I needed much more. My spirit was hungry and lacking real nourishment. My fast food approach to life was unhealthy and killing me.

AS I began the process of getting to know who I truly was without all the stuff. I disappeared from the public, and I became obsessed with research on healing my mind, body, and spirit. I was ready to do the work needed to get me out of this repetitive slump I was in. I learned how to meditate and started spending a lot of time in silence. I began reading empowerment books, watching inspirational shows and practicing affirmations.

The more I fed my spirit, the hungrier it got. I began to get excited about learning new things. There was so much more out there to explore and expand my awareness beyond what I knew or had been taught. My spirit began to glow immensely; my eyes brightened as I became more aware and clear. I began to feel safe again in my own skin.

Finally, I was retrieving pieces of my soul and finding my smile again. Ultimately, people started to notice and say things like, "There's something really different about you. I never realized how beautiful you are." But it wasn't really that I had changed much on the outside. I was the same size and weight but with less of everything from makeup to hair and just stuff. The positive comments were coming so frequently that I would often look in the mirror to see what had changed. Then I had an Aha moment, it was my spirit that was glowing. That is what they saw; they just couldn't pinpoint it. People began to treat me differently, more gentle, more loving, more respectful.

Even folks that I had known for years seemed to want to get to know me on a deeper, more psychological level, they wanted to hear what I had to say. At first I was apprehensive and protective, but I embraced it. I had become okay with simply being myself, allowing my confidence to bask in humility, gratefulness and compassion. I also began to trust myself and the decisions I made when it came to feeling people out. I spent less time in the mirror and more time with myself, quietly healing and developing spiritually away from everything I had known for many years.

AFTER moving back to LA, I was tested, and survived another one of life's heart-wrenching lessons. I didn't realize it at the time, but I was catapulted into alignment of purpose. I found myself in a place of re-evaluation again. Homeless, in a motel with my son, feeling suicidal & desperately trying to get myself together. Although I didn't have the money to buy new clothes, I no longer wanted to sit around looking or feeling sorry for myself.

I then began to hear the whispers in my spirit telling me "It's bigger than you, you're going through this for someone else. Get up, you have more to do, it's not over." I decided from that day forward I'm not going to keep going through this BS. I'm gonna get up and really get my shit together." By this point I was angry, I had been here way too many times. The buck would stop here! I would get my swag back and continue it for the rest of my life. I know what needs to be done, I'm creative, I have great ideas and I'm gonna do them ALL! One by one, sometimes two by two, I'm going to make it happen for ME! I'm changing my story - because I can.

After meeting the psychiatrist and feeling a lot better. I

immediately went to my motel and started cleaning it up, I put my favorite flowers around the room, brought my comforter and pillows from out of my car and set the table to look like something other than an old dingy box. I lit some of my vanilla scented candles, saged the room and began being grateful for what I had. I had to put into action all that I had learned over the last few years. Here's a few pictures from that day.

Oct 2012 - Before pic

so filthy

Our motel on Hollywood blvd

Home

Is where you make it!

I began to be grateful for what we did have and gave it love.

After pic

201

our kitchen

A s far as looks goes, I didn't have extra money for my hair, so I would neatly pull it back in a cute little bun. I had finally become confident enough to do that. When I was younger

I was told to never show a man my real hair, because he would never get that picture out of his mind. I know this sounds extremely nuts, but many young girls are taught this because that is what their parents were taught; as if doing so would make them less appealing.

I never unveiled my natural hair until it began falling out due to lack of blood flow where my brain avm was. Interestingly enough as I began to embrace my natural beauty; the dependency on my weaves to be deemed attractive dissipated. More importantly, I began appealing to incredible, brilliant men who thought I was just as beautiful either way. Nowadays, if I wear a weave it's no longer because it defines me, but because I feel like it! I even opted for more natural makeup looks. I also threw out all of my faded and old clothing. I was determined that if I had to wear the same black tank, jeans and heels with a suit jacket every day until I got it together, I would do just that!

I worked with what I had. And you know what? I started attracting money. Because I looked like I cared about myself and my energy exuded excitement about building my business and being really good at what I do. I focused on what I wanted instead of what I was lacking. I then got myself an apartment, and I told myself I would get a studio, because I felt that was the only way to be taken seriously in this business, and nine months later it happened. At first, I had no portfolio, but I worked at it, perfecting my craft and landed my first celebrity magazine cover shoot a month after opening my doors. I was getting my swag back. Even now as a Television Producer, I just started creating ideas and filming them. I became clear about what I wanted, and I put it out there. Now I'm producing shows for networks like HBO and CMT.

MY confidence grew rapidly when I began I doing things for me. Not waiting on someone to hand it to me, but making it happen by changing the way I think, being prepared, and always open to learning more. And when God said I was ready, he threw a huge splash of favor over me. During harder times, I also made sure to work on my inner glow, my spirit. I began to listen to spiritual tapes while I was working, as well as spending a lot of time alone, even taking myself on dates to get to know me. I made sure to keep my nails and toes manicured because I felt better about myself when they were done even if that meant doing it myself. I would meditate in the bath, started stretching daily when I couldn't work out, (which I'm still not that good at.) But I did it for me! Not for anyone else.

When I glance at myself in the mirror, I now embrace the positive changes and give myself a compliment instead of focusing on the negatives. I even became a pescatarian. It did something spiritually to me that made me less heavy and mentally more clear. It was important for me to be healthy in every way. Oh and I don't go outside looking a mess ever, nor do I sit around in private that way. Every day, I must at least comb my hair into a bun, and it has lifted me out of many funky moods.

There are several incredible women in business that I respect and look up to as I watch and study them. They embody strength, poise, confidence and balance. People like Kimora Lee Simmons, Jada Pinkett Smith, Oprah Winfrey, Beyonce Knowles and Angelina Jolie. I would often ask myself would they go out looking like they just rolled out of bed; or allow themselves to be treated in a negative, disrespectful or unprofessional way. Absolutely not! So I model my life after what they represent for the type of woman I am becoming.

I also want to note that they are powerful women that are bosses who run their own companies. They have something of their own going on. I needed that fulfillment.

Something that I did for myself. Also, I started getting rid of the clutter that was holding my emotions hostage. It's really important that you detach yourself from THINGS. The only way for you to be blessed with more is if you have the space for it. No matter what it is. It could be love, clothes, friends, a spouse, a job; it doesn't matter. Every now and then you need to get rid of things and people that no longer serve a purpose in your life. There should not be stuff piled in every corner of your home. Closets filled to the ceiling or spilling out the door with things you only 'hope' to wear again one day. Get rid of that stuff, you're holding yourself up. It's time to CLEANSE everything, physically, mentally and spiritually. Let it go! You can do it! Not later, Now.

GET yourself together and stop running around looking a mess, half done, with wraps and bonnets on your hair or inappropriate clothing, wondering why people are repelled by you. Re-assess what you are putting out there and you will discover why people aren't treating you with the respect you deserve. I know we're busy, but we have to make time to care.

What are some changes you can make to recalibrate your swag? Let's start with getting rid of stuff you don't need or use. If you haven't touched it in 9-10 months, its time for it to go in the goodwill bin. Remember things carry energy; that's why many of us are suffocating and can't see our way to a new level of living.

Write down in order, the areas of your life that you are going to start decluttering. For me, I started with my clothes, and then I moved on to all the papers and photos I had stacked in drawers and bins from years ago. Things I was unconsciously, unwilling and afraid to let go of. Baggage from stuff that I had been lugging around from place to place for many years.

Soul Exercise

• Think of 3 places you will begin to declutter in your life. For instance, your bedroom drawers, closets, phone book, office, old pictures and memories, etc.

• On the next page, make a list of things that you can choose to do for yourself. Once a week pick 1 thing off of your list to do.

Love on Me List

List things that make you smile or feel good about yourself.

Pick

Something off your list once a week as a gift or treat to yourself.

You deserve it!

Chapter Sixteen

FLAWS AND ALL

AS I have gotten older, I've realized and accepted that there is such a magnificent beauty in our flaws. It's what makes you unique and special. For so long I was told that I wasn't good enough, pretty enough, talented enough, smart enough, light or dark enough and the lists goes on.

I was always the oddball in the group even as a young child and it carried into adulthood causing major insecurities and a constant need for validity and acceptance. It seemed I was always the circle trying to force myself into a square hole. I had all these ideas and brilliant thoughts of things that no one ever really understood. I saw everything so differently from most around me. And what may have seemed as me being a rebel, was simply just the courage to do what others wouldn't, I challenged what most labeled as impossible. So I was deemed by some as insane or living in a naive bubble. I was never really told that I was smart and I never felt as if I belonged anywhere really.

Now living in Hollywood can make you pick yourself part to the point you lose touch with who you really are completely. I presumed I was flawed and that made me automatically a failure with big dreams. Unconsciously; I use to sabotage myself without even knowing it. I was never good enough because that is what other people stamped on me as a child. That is what I believed in my heart even though I said otherwise and it continued into adulthood.

Today I know better, as I am always striving to accept

and understand myself better. To acknowledge and notice the little things about myself and my personality that are unique and be ok with that; which helps me to love myself more.

AT some point, you have to love on the parts of you that others make you feel guilty for. You have to embrace the beauty in those so-called flaws and see yourself as 'flaws-less' as Beyonce would say.

Something magical happens when you no longer bear the weight or have a need for other people's opinions to feed or tear down your ego and esteem. When you no longer need to be in places or with people that you don't even like in order to feel important or secure because of status or whatever excuse you've conjured up or been brain washed into believing. When you no longer need to attach yourself to anyone to make you into the incredible man or woman you are to become. That moment when you embrace and take back your power by realizing that you are enough just as you are.

When will you decided to no longer hide or dim your light in order to make other people feel more comfortable in their skin or position. See, I made a decision that I would no longer accept or be on the receiving end of other people's bullshit. They may say that I've changed, but like Jay Z said "I didn't work this hard to stay the same." I now take away people's right to speak to me or be in my presence if they refuse to treat me respectfully like the beautiful person that I am. No longer will I allow myself to be disrespected or give a pass to people because that's just how they are. Thinking it's cute or funny. I don't allow myself to laugh off ignorance anymore. Because it's not funny. You know those types that get away with everything and call it just kidding.

I AM

no longer afraid to speak up or occasionally tell someone to 'get the hell on' if need be and never look back. I no longer play the role with someone by allowing them to do and say whatever they want upon meeting me. Or even the influential men and or women that often try to touch or do inappropriate things with no lead on, because they feel they can. Meanwhile, you're stuck and uncomfortable trying to dodge them and be nice so that you don't miss out on a business opportunity.

Recently, I was told by a great friend and mentor of mine, 'Chris Hicks' (Former VP of Def Jam) who has always challenged me intellectually to dig deeper and really access things from a broader perspective. He said, "You don't lose opportunities that way. Either you have the opportunity or you don't. You don't have to play nice when it comes to inappropriate acts, nor do you have to deal with the bullshit no matter who they are. You need to speak up right then. If you lose the 'supposed' opportunity, it was never there to begin with." I immediately was like wow, he's right. What am I doing? I believe a lot of that thinking came from what I was taught over the years as a woman; to play the role otherwise men would never allow me to get ahead in this industry. It was like I had to accept it and try to maneuver through their immaturity, disrespect; power trips and extremely aggressive sexual advances to be allowed to move forward. But that wasn't true at all.

So I decided to create my own opportunities without needing to go through anyone or play any games. I started my own company and did my own thing, and they came to me. Like a popular scripture says. "Your gift will make room from you." I believe that now more than ever.

In my personal life, I believe it was something similar. I have been neglected and disrespected by many men, women, and family members, yet preceded to take the silence is golden high road. But eventually my good heart would let the wrong people back in, and once again I'm hurt, torn down and emotionally; taking a beating to where I can't even focus on my life. Why? Because I had accepted that I was flawed in the worst way. Never good enough for anything. I completely understand that people who hurt people are hurting and they need the most love; because essentially somewhere in their life; they are missing something. But that doesn't mean that you have to allow them to beat up on you while they get they're act together. Some people need to be loved from a distance, or need to be shut off completely as you gracefully wave goodbye.

I've also found that there are many folks who hate on you because they see your potential, and are envious of who they think you may become. They will for no good reason cause all kind of unnecessary havoc in your life. Any chance that they get to hurt you and they go for the gusto, saying and doing things that cut so deep they feel virtually unforgivable. All the while you're sitting there wondering what the hell did I do to you, or I don't deserve to be treated this way? But the major kicker is, this wasn't new. I am willing to bet that these hurtful things have been happening with this person for a long time. But you go along with it, because you're trying to stick around for whatever reason. Could be the kids, could be your insecurity of being alone, could be your lack of self-worth or guilt. Whatever the reason, you know that this is nothing new to you. You shouldn't even be surprised anymore. Yet, you're left emotionally scarred, hurt and angry constantly because you let the guilt of your good heart, convince you they were going to be someone other than who they really are.

Tyrese said something so powerful one day; "Stop hanging out with pain and giving people emotional access to you. At some point, your loyalty has to have an expiration date when bullshit people reveal themselves. Stop investing time with people who tear you down, or throw your past in your face every chance they get to hurt you.

Your past does not define your future. You are worth your weight in diamonds. You are authentic and beautifully made. You are here for a purpose. Sadly for some and almost for me at one point you go through so much that you just want to end it all. Life can sometimes make you feel as if no one cares as you're constantly beat up and tossed from one bad or hurtful situation to the next; that you just want everything to stop, and that includes life.

I was there, many times. But I get it now. You are here for a purpose just like everyone else. You are important to someone. You are a essential piece to this gigantic puzzle of life and all of us are scrambling to figure out where we fit. Don't give up on you!

I also just want to clarify for some of you. Being famous or having a prominent title, that does not always correspond with success. Society has somehow convinced us that being rich and famous, having a big house an extravagant car or having a grandiose title in a company is somehow the status quo that we are all trying to reach in order to be happy, validated, confident, powerful, successful and looked at as flawless or perfect. But if that was the case why are so many famous or influential "perfect" people who seemingly have everything, killing themselves constantly? It's because there is no real spiritual fulfillment, no real joy or true sense of self. Somehow it gets lost along the way. I know some of the most successful people that are so depressed and confused when they are not the center of everyone's attention or at the top of the charts. I have always been shocked to find out when I asked the deeper questions, or when you strip away the titles, and flashy things; many of them are some of the most insecure, empty people you have ever met. Many have lost touch with reality because they constantly try to keep up with the facade of who they think others expect them to be. Most are even in debt trying to appear like they're 'ballin', but really struggling to pay the simplest bills. They are hurting just like you and I. Many are just confused, trying to figure out why they have this emptiness that seems to just linger or creep in and out when they least expect it. Not realizing, it's a lack of true fulfillment, purpose, and taking the time to figure out who they really are.

I hear so many people say, "when I make it, I'm gonna this and that..." Ok, so you make it - whatever that means to you! Now what? Those are the questions we need to all be asking. You could be the best pie maker in the world and make people smile, or you could be a nanny who helps raise incredible children, those may seem small but those are gifts. That is still a form of success.

I remember one day I had a conversation with another mentor of mine; a very prominent, well respected, intelligent, successful man by the name of 'Jeff Johnson' (well known as a BET & CNN correspondent). I contacted him on social media because I was in awe of how he use to go to different countries during disasters to help people, as well as cover the stories. I spoke to him around the time when Haiti had that massive earthquake and my spirit was yearning for something more, I so badly wanted to help in a hands on way. I said to him, "I can't wait to become a successful singer that way I can really help people, go to different countries and physically be there lending a hand and it really matter. I really want to make a difference in people's lives, that is my purpose." He said, "I don't understand that, why aren't you doing that now, why do you have to wait until you're famous to reach people? There are so many ways to help out, so many organizations that you can work with to do just that" You don't need fame to make an impact in lives of people." That conversation really made me think. It seemed to almost changed me instantly. And since then, I changed my perception and definition of what success actually was. What was I doing? Was I waiting on some sort of approval, for people to give me some kind of validation or green light that said I was powerful or good enough? I don't know. But it changed the way I looked at my accessibility to help others.

There also came the moment when I stopped caring so much about hanging out with everybody or being everywhere just to make myself feel important. I released having pointless prominent people in my phone. Or being so concerned with keeping up with what everyone was wearing, trying to live up to what I was expected to look, act, dress, talk and pretend to be like.

That was the moment I believe, I became beautiful to me. I was ok just being home doing the things I liked that made me happy; even if that meant watching TV or spending time with my son. Even something simple like calling some of my girls over, cooking dinner and having movie night. I became so much more peaceful and less heavy. My spirit began to flourish as I stopped doing things I simply didn't like to do, or being around people I didn't really like, as well as passing on places that drained or made me feel uncomfortable. I surrounded myself with love. There I felt safe, uplifted, respected and embraced. It was there in those blissful moments that I began to see myself and learned to look at my so-called flaws a bit differently. I could look at a dimple in my thigh and laugh instead of obsessing about how imperfect it was. It was in those moments of feeling safe that I got a clear view of my real personality. Like how I was actually quite a bit silly with an interesting sense of humor that I never allowed anyone to see. I got to wear my real hair and still feel beautiful with no judgment. It's amazing how much there is to love when you allow yourself to just be.

I came to the conclusion while in those beautiful moments with myself and the people I loved; that in the past, I was most likely depressed all the time because I didn't like my representative! The person that sought perfection and invited nonconstructive criticism and self hate to herself. I was bored and disgusted with the girl I had turned myself into, based off what I thought I was suppose to be. I lacked depth and never executed any real purpose, outside of my own selfish goals to be wanted, admired and famous so that I could fill that void of emptiness. That girl depressed me. There was nothing exciting or fullfilling about her. But I always knew deep down there was more. I just needed to find it.

I remember the moment I changed my name to Phoenix; which means to "rise from the ashes." I decided it was time for me to wake up. And although it has taken me quite a few years to get to this point, I am so grateful that I did. Because now I am comfortable in my skin and don't really care what people think about it. It's so less stressful.

I wake up every day excited about what I do. Excited about fulfilling my purpose, and I can actually say I like me a lot. No, everybody may not get me, or understand me and that's ok. But I get me. I feel free. Free of guilt, free of shame, free of self-hatred. I am no longer afraid to love, and I've given myself permission to be loved by others. I'm also not afraid to be hurt, nor do I expect it. I just live. I'm ok with being completely honest with myself and the people around me. And you know what? I now attract the most amazingly beautiful spirited people to my life. The kind of people that are constantly showing me how to love and receive love in different ways.

I embrace being a woman and all the elements that come with it. I'm no longer afraid to express my sexuality, intelligence, creativity, sensitivity, beauty, brains or power. I'm ok with sounding a bit silly if it's what I feel or believe, no longer fearing standing up for myself. I no longer feel as if I lack something when I'm single. Nor do I completely lose myself when I'm in love. I allow myself to feel what I feel, and I express it without feeling sorry about what I do or don't like. I'm honest with people; no longer feeling the pressure to play a game to get what I want. I'm open to vulnerability, as I no longer consider it to be a weakness, but a strength that's more beautiful than anything. I take better care of my heart and trust myself to protect it from what others throw at me in an effort to derail my emotions.

I can now smile and mean it with all of my heart. Because I am now comfortable in my own skin flaws and all. My imperfections are perfection in my eyes. And whatever I need to work on I grow and evolve spiritually, mentally, and physically to make me a better me; I am willing to do the work. I am the writer of my story. As I have turned my pain into a triumph and testimony that evokes healing in others. I thank God for making me just as I am.

IT'S TIME to make some real grown up

decisions in your life. Ask yourself; who am I without all the stuff? What is my purpose? What am I good at? What would I love to do if given the opportunity?

Then list some of amazing things you love about yourself! For me, part of my purpose it to plant seeds in the minds and hearts of people to empower, inspire and ultimately help them to heal.

What I *Love* About Me

_____

_____

_____

_____

_____

_____

_____

_____

_____

_____

_____

_____

_____

_____

_____

_____

_____

_____

_____

_____

_____

Whatever
you don't water,
will die

Chapter Seventeen

THE POWER OF
INTENTION & FLOW

How does a person go from being homeless to being wealthy mentally, physically, spiritually and emotionally in very little time? The answer lies in the power of intention. I have seen some of the most amazing things happen to my life in an instant when I am fully operating in the power of intention and flow. Enemies have become friends; hate turned into love, and an overdraft bank account to having more zeros than anyone in my family had ever seen at one time by simply shifting my thoughts and feelings.

For a long time I didn't realize that I had been doing this unconsciously for a while as my life yo-yo'd up and down constantly. What I've come to realize, is that most of our minds work on autopilot, which has somehow been programmed to think the absolute worst in almost every situation. Hence, the reason we have such a high rate of people feeling stressed; which is also causing many of us to be sick starting at a young age. Many of us are so overwhelmed with fear and hopelessness; because we spend the majority of our time thinking about what we lack instead of what we love.

But let me let you in on a little secret. Everything that is happening in your life right now, you are attracting it. It's all about the vibrational signal that you are sending out good and bad. Your vibration stems from your thoughts and feelings no matter what. You simply can't fool the Universe. It always knows the truth.

For instance; when you complain or are always stressed about all your bills. The signal you are sending out is that you want more bills. You will find things start to shift in your life in order to create more bills for you; because that's all you think about. The universe gives you exactly what you want; by what you feel, think and say. If you want more love, give more love, spend time thinking about what that looks and feels like. Not the catastrophe and fear from your last relationship, or what you don't want to happen.

You must spend time every day visualizing the end result of what you want, and what that feels like. What does it look and feel like to be successful in your dream career? What does receiving a check to pay all your bills for the amazing services that are provided to you to make your life better; like electricity or the roof over your head. You have to get excited about paying your bills instead of dreading them. You should be grateful to pay for the home that protects you, the hot water and electricity that we use to take a shower and power our devices. And if you don't have the money to pay them right now. Stop over thinking about it, create a payment plan, communicate, work it out. I know I sound a bit crazy to some of you, but I am only speaking from the experience of what has shifted me out of poverty and lack.

I compare money similar to that of a puppy. The more you chase it; the more it runs from you. But ignore it, and go about doing your own thing and the puppy will come to find you wanting to play. Same thing with money, focus on passion and purpose, do your part, and the money will find you. That's not saying quit your jobs and don't take care of your responsibilities. But what I am saying is stop worrying so much about something you can't do anything about. What's the point! Your time and thoughts are better spent elsewhere for your sake. Otherwise you are throwing rocks on your own road, ultimately delaying your miracle.

I have witnessed time and time again, when I set my intention on any particular thing I want; more times than not, I get it. That is unless it's simply just not for me. Being in alignment mixed with the power of intention is a beautiful spot to be in. It will often leaves you saying "wow, did that really just happen." I have these miraculous moments almost every day. You see, setting your intention is merely just daydreaming with a purpose. It's using your imagination to raise your vibration into a higher realm to the point you actually feel the magic and energy happening in that very moment. That is where you want to be.

Whatever it is that you may want or need, make sure you are feeling and operating as if you already have it. By that, I mean feeling the joy, confidence and vitality that comes with having what you want. As well as taking some sort of action. You must learn to walk in a state of knowing. In the bible, there's a popular verse that says "Faith is the substance of things hoped for and the evidence of things not seen." To me that means knowing something is going to happen. Most people get stuck in merely just hoping. That is not true faith, because saying you hope something happens leaves doubt, whereas saying, I know something is going to work out is a totally different feeling.

During my days under the Christian faith, I found myself constantly praying over and over for the same things while calling it having faith. But it wasn't faith at all; it was fear that God might not do what I prayed for the first time. But most of us don't realize that we are not operating on true faith we are operating mostly on fear. Right now, no matter what spiritual religion you practice; I say it's time we shake things up a bit and began to reprogram our minds. I personally have flashes of hundreds of negative things every day with loads of fear and deterring thoughts that try to come creeping in to throw me off my path. But I always do my best to counteract them with something positive. I say little things like "I cancel that out", especially when I get thoughts of bad things happening, or those arguments that you have with people all in your head. I have learned to shift my thoughts to create an alternate outcome that I want or simply stop worrying about it and allow the universe to work out my problem as it sees fit. As long as I stay focused on the end result, I don't care how I get there. I just know what I want, I get very specific and leave room for miracles to happen by not trying to control every little step. Which I call living in the state of the unknown. Better known as, to surrender.

Again, you must be very clear with what you want when it comes to certain things. If you are not clear; it's highly likely whatever you get back won't be either; this step is absolutely crucial.

In addition to that, I have found that my words are extremely powerful. Be very careful about the way you vent to others or the things that you say. For instance; things like "somebody is always taking advantage of me", "everyone always hurts me", "just trying to pay all these bills" and the oh so familiar "I'm broke". You have to stop it because you will get exactly that. Try making a habit of saying today is gonna be an amazing day. I often say "something amazing is gonna happen to me today" and I smile, and more times than not, something does. I even do it with my son. When I drive or walk him to school I always ask "what is today gonna be?" And he screams out with enthusiasm, "A Great Day!" That way he is also setting his intention on having a great day at school.

Another powerful way of taking intention to the next level is to faithfully act on it. For instance; those of you that want a man or a woman in your life, try acting as if you already have one. Leave a bit of space in your closet for them, clean up your house as if he or she was coming home to you. Are you going out every weekend? Try staying home, sitting in front of the fireplace with a glass of wine or doing something of that nature and be happy about it.

Think of what it would be like to share that moment with someone you love. Try sleeping on one side of the bed. What are you wearing to bed? How are you taking care of your home or yourself for that matter? Live as if you already have what you want or as if you're expecting it any minute now.

Act as if you already have it, not as if you lack it; and watch how some of the most amazing things, people, and experiences begin to happen in your life. That is, if you're ready. Start opening up your heart to be loved. Get rid of exes and past relationships that you are no longer with, yet they are still occupying space in your heart. Because I know first hand that you can be single, but your heart be taken. For those of you wanting more money; clean out your junky purses or wallets filled with old receipts and cards you don't use. Make space for the money to go in. Also get rid of some of the miscellaneous bills that you are wasting your money on, so that it can start to trust you again to be responsible with it. Make some room in your house and closets to receive more. Many of us are out of space. Nothing else can fit anywhere. Release some of that stuff taking up all that space and get organized. You have to start preparing for success. Dress like you are successful already. I for one had to go out and buy a bunch of button up blouses and blazers to go with my jeans. I realized, I wasn't dressing like a successful business woman, so for a while there I wasn't attracting it either.

At one point I was only attracting people who were struggling, looking for a handout or expecting a hookup. I wasn't respected. Once I made a few minor changes, I felt different, and people started valuing me as such. Only then did I started attracting a more lucrative business flow. I will give you a prime example of intention & flow. I really wanted to be a producer and director, but no one would give me the opportunity to do it on a high level, so I begin to visualize what that looked like. I pictured producing big shows on set, working on what I loved. Then I put it in to action; as I started creating and directing little short films, music videos, and TV shows for myself as if it was being made for a network, with excellence.

Little did I know, I would end up on a reality show within a month or so. That led to me meeting the president of a major production company that created it. I told him; "Watch I'm coming to work with you." And he said ok, we can have a meeting when we wrap. Everyday on set, I would map out and compartmentalize every facet of this huge production. I would literally get excited breathing in the very energy of it all. I wanted it! I deserved it, and I believed it was possible because I was confident in what I had to offer. I just needed to be given an opportunity in a big way.

After we wrapped a month later, I scheduled a meeting with and showed the president of the company my work. After the meeting, I started to feel that I needed to get rid of some things in preparation for something big. One of those things being to close my studio that I only had for a year, something I was incredibly apprehensive about, but I went with the flow. Literally 20 min after I turned in my keys closing my studio, I got a call from the production company asking if I was available to be a story producer for a new show on Country Music Television and that I needed to leave the next day for up to a month. I was like "wow, did that really just happen!" So I went with the flow. Even though I had been my own boss and CEO. I was like a sponge, I remained humble while learning everything I could on the job with very little direction. Which in most cases, all you have to do is really listen to the people, conversations and actions around you. That way it becomes easy to catch on. I then came home from that job and got a call to be a producer for an HBO show 2 weeks later, and would need to leave immediately. I just went with the flow and ended up not only becoming one of the main producers, but also as a director in several segments of the new series.

What I learned from that; was not to ask, pray, or visualize the steps to getting there. But to simply focus on the end result. That way you leave room for miracles to happen and don't hold yourself up by trying to control how you get there. And as the pieces start to shift in to place, be flexible and go with the flow. The most amazing people and opportunities will flow into your life effortlessly.

Your thoughts and emotions can destroy or make your life incredible. Many of us don't realize that once we reclaim power over just our thoughts and get a hold of our emotions; it builds a confidence and strength in us that no one can shake. But please note, it's an everyday choice that you have to make.

• I am challenging you to get a few pieces of paper and make a list in the different areas of your life. What does your happy life picture look like? Now don't make it too-complicated because this will change and evolve as you continue to grow.

• Then take five min a day and spend time with that picture, visualizing and really feeling it.

• Lastly, you must make at least one action towards creating that happy life picture everyday. If your everyday actions are not in line with what truly makes you happy, then that is where you're going wrong. You will ultimately never experience true joy, bliss and fulfillment if nothing in your life reflects what it is you truly want. Instead of what you've settled for.

Redefining strong is about taking back your life and thoughts, by not letting them control you anymore, which have been hindering and destroying your progress as well as your dreams. So if you're ready to move forward. This is one of the main ways to do it. Change your thoughts, change your words, change your feelings, put it into action and you will change your life. The more excited you get, the more empowered you feel, the faster you begin to attract it to you.

Visualization

What does your happy life picture look like. Not what you're willing to settle for. When you think of your perfect career, what does that look like? Be specific. Close your eyes and think about the following questions.

- What are you doing?
- What does your environment look like?
- What do you look like?
- How does this position make you feel about yourself?
- How are other people reacting to you?

Repeat this visualization technique in all the major areas of your life. Health and Body Image, Finances, Relationships, etc. The purpose is to get a clear vision, that way you spend time with that picture instead of being all over the place or unclear.

Chapter Eighteen

HOW TO LOVE YOU...
BETTER

L ike I've said before in a previous chapter. I use to always get so annoyed when people would tell me that I needed to love myself, but no one ever showed me or told me how. Aside from the fact that I generally thought I was. No one sat me down and taught me any different. I had to learn the hard way through trial and error, as well as a bit of research and spiritual development. I've written down a quick list of ways you can begin to start loving yourself more, so that we all can begin to paint a true, honest picture of what it really is.

01 | TAKE CARE OF YOUR BODY

What many of us don't realize is that our physical health also plays an enormous role in our mental well-being. It also plays a pivotal role in how we feel when we look in the mirror, as well as our confidence and self-esteem. It's not about dieting or getting skinny to fit the mold that society has placed on us; it's about feeling good from the inside out. Many of us are walking sewage tanks, with years of build up and toxins that are affecting our everyday lives. Trust me, when you change your diet everything changes; you even become more clear spiritually. There is no way you can say you love yourself – or your body - if you are feeding it things that will eventually hurt you or cause you to be sick or dependent on medication in the long run. That is not love. Listen to your body and what it needs.

02 | ALLOW YOURSELF TO FEEL WHAT YOU FEEL

When you're going through something, allow yourself to feel what you feel without judgment, and then let it pass through you. When you don't release emotions the way the body naturally wants to, by trying to hide or mask it; eventually that discomfort, sadness, and pain gets trapped inside of you and becomes a trigger waiting for someone to push it - then you explode. (Or even worse - implode.) So just breathe, take a moment and allow whatever you are feeling to pass through you, so it doesn't get trapped in you.

03 | RELEASE YOURSELF OF GUILT & SHAME

Whatever mistakes you have made in the past are just that, in the past. At some point, you have to get over it. You are not your past; you are not your mistakes. They are simply the lessons you needed in order to move forward. The quicker you can release what was, the faster you can become the incredible person you are truly meant to be. All you have to do is make a choice to no longer use or allow the guilt & shame from whatever or whomever as a punishment to keep you from the life and love you deserve. It is what it is. S**t happens. It's a part of life. Everybody has a skeleton closet, everybody has something they are ashamed of or feels guilty about, and I mean EVERYBODY don't tell yourself any different. It is impossible to create the future by clinging to the past.

04 | BE PATIENT WITH YOURSELF

Stop comparing yourself, your relationships, and your accomplishments to everyone else's deadline, opinion, plan, or vision. Don't place time limits on when things have to happen for you in order for you to be happy. I know so many who believe they have to be married by a certain age, or they feel like a failure. It's unrealistic and unhealthy. Allow the universe to bring you to where you're suppose to be, when you're suppose to be there. Otherwise, forcing a door open in the wrong timing can cause a major disaster. There's no hurry. Like I always say, just walk in flow and allow things to happen organically.

05 | STAND UP FOR YOURSELF

Speak up, be brave, stand up for what you believe in with confidence, and don't make any excuses or apologies for it. It's time out for allowing people to trample all over to you, by doing, saying and treating you however they see fit. It's ok to say NO! Stand up for yourself - gracefully of course, LOL.

06 | MEDITATE

Spend time in silence; take a moment each day to make time for yourself. I do this often at night in the bath where I light candles and play soft meditation music. I also do it first thing in the morning to balance and ground myself before I take on my day. It's important to quiet your mind and mouth so that you can connect with your spirit, clear your mind and listen. It's also extremely relaxing.

07 | DO WHAT YOU LOVE

Make time to do things that you love to do. Whether it's creating something based on the idea; visiting a place you have always wanted to go to, painting, maybe even writing a book - do it! Stop making excuses for why you don't have the time to do things for you, when you make time to do everything for everyone else. Make you important. Do what you love. Life is too short to keep procrastinating. Also, it will bring you incredible fulfillment and joy when you complete something that meant something special to you.

08 | SURRENDER TO THE UNKNOWN

Allow yourself to be in the moment, ego-less, without judgment or worry from the past and without anxious thoughts about the future. Surrender to the moment, without the need or struggle to control everything due to fear. Just be and allow the universe to surprise you. There's something magical about living fearlessly in a state of the unknown.

09 | ALLOW OTHERS TO HELP YOU

Loving yourself is not always trying to do everything by yourself. Sometimes you need help, allow others to help you. It could be as simple as someone offering to carry a bag for you that is too heavy for you to drag upstairs. It could be hiring a housekeeper to help clean up because you're unable to get everything done after working all day. Or even asking a friend or family member to help out with something, (which most of us have too much pride to do.) Stop feeling bad about not being superhuman or getting into a jam. And listen; if someone offers to take care of something financially, don't push away the blessing you were asking God for because of ego. Allow someone to help you.

10 | GRATITUDE

Learn to be grateful for everything around you. The people in your life, the gas in your car, the home that you live in and even the lessons that you've learned. Also don't forget to express your gratitude, appreciation and love to those around you. It not only lifts their spirit, but it will also lift yours. Not to mention; gratitude and appreciation intensifies your vibration sending signals into the universe to bring more things into your life to be grateful for.

11 | LET GO OF TOXIC PEOPLE

I heard someone say that you become like the five people you spend the most time with. What type of people are you around the most? Are the closest people in your life negative, or are they inspiring? Do they build you up or are they constantly judging you and tearing you down? The release of toxins is a necessary step in developing a healthy life – this includes toxic people.

12 | DO SOMETHING NICE FOR YOURSELF

Show yourself how you want to be treated or loved. Buy yourself flowers, or take yourself on a trip. Get a massage every now and then. Take yourself out for dinner and order whatever you want, maybe even try something new. Don't wait for someone else to make you feel special or do something that you can do for yourself. Love on you.

13 | AFFIRMATIONS

Words are powerful; start speaking love and life over yourself. I've written an affirmation to help with self-love. You can write it on a piece of paper or your mirror. It is totally up to you. Repeat it to yourself as often as you like.

14. | GIVE BACK TO THOSE IN NEED

You'd be surprised how amazing you feel after you spend time helping those in need. It instantly puts things into perspective and evokes an incredible amount of gratitude and spiritual fulfillment. Grab those clothes you bagged up and take them to a shelter. Or possible get someone some food and a little bit of your time. It goes such a long way.

SELF-LOVE
Affirmations

I am a beautiful person,

I am lovable person

I am wonderfully made with purpose

I am whole

I am bold

I am loved

I am free

I am enough

I am capable of anything I set my mind to

I am excited about my future

I am worth my weight in diamonds

I Thank you God for making me just as I am

I love me

Chapter Nineteen

FOLLOW THE WHISPER

Along this journey of life we're given guides. The soft whispers in our spirit that many have deemed our conscious, deja vu, spirit guides, angels or the holy spirit. Most commonly we've all heard the small voice that told us to turn left or right. To slow down or stop with no real reason or explanation. Sometimes we listen and sometimes we ignore it. This soft whisper is our inner navigational system that's here to guide you along your life's journey, but most times we just don't listen. And that is where many of us have gone wrong, and ended up lost or extremely far from our destination while run down and out of gas because we just didn't listen. How many times have you said to yourself, "Man I knew that was gonna happen? Or I should have just followed my first mind or just went with my first instinct?"

A lot of times instead of listening we talk ourselves out of doing what were being led to do. Most times because it doesn't seem to make a lot of sense from our standpoint. Or, it doesn't seem logical, possible or convenient. I have made this mistake so many times and the repercussions and learning lessons have been the worst.

At this point in my life, I do my best to listen almost always as the whispers for me get louder the more I follow and acknowledge them. It's to the point sometimes that I don't even need to hear it more than once because I can actually feel it with all of my being. Minus a few slip ups here and there where I could've saved myself some headache and heartache, but I chose to be hard headed.

A good example of following the whisper, would be when I was living in Atlanta. My spirit told me that I would be moving back to LA to finish what I had started. And of course I was like, "I'm not moving anywhere." Plus, I couldn't afford that and too much pain lived there. So, as I was meditating and automatic writing, (where I get in a quiet place to connect spiritually; then I write the words 'Listening' in my journal and I wait for whatever I hear; and then write word for word whatever message I get or visions I see.)

ONE DAY I heard that I was moving back to

LA in one week which was a Sat. I was like there's no way! I had no money, I hadn't even paid my roommate yet for my portion of the rent and my account was overdrawn. On top of that, my license had just expired. So driving cross country seemed crazy and impossible.

I was then told (while listening to my spirit) I would get $5,000 from a specific company that I had done design work for, and that I had to make a list of everything I needed to make the trip and price it out to the exact dollar amount. So I said ok; if the money comes, I will go. Otherwise, I'm not going anywhere. So I began to pack and put stuff in my car just in case the money showed up.

Now of course I had nowhere to live in LA, no plan, no work, nothing. All of a sudden I began to notice the shift beginning. That same week my roommate told me I would have to move out by the 1st, which was a week away or her property manager would start getting upset that I wasn't on the lease. I'm thinking "ok, what am I gonna do?" I continued to pack anyway. Out of nowhere; Thursday comes and I receive a retainer of $5,000 for design work from the exact company I was told I would. So I said, I guess I'm moving to LA. So I went and got everything I needed on my list. Tires checked, paid my rent, and figured hey, I'll just leave Friday, no point in waiting, but that night I booked a headshot shoot for Friday and couldn't leave till Sat. The exact day I was told a week prior. The whisper was right on point. So as I'm driving to Los Angeles I start seeing 11:11 the whole time repeating everywhere I went. Literally every time I looked at the clock, temperature or signs it was there. I realized I had just clicked into alignment by simply listening and trusting the unknown. It was and still is a daily sign that I see that let's me know that I'm on track. 11-11-14 which will also be the exact date I launch this book.

So as I'm driving my dad says you should stop in Miami and get your stuff out of storage. So I took a detour, rented a huge hitch, found some movers on Craigslist to load my two bedroom storage in the trailer and I drove it by myself all the way to LA. I had no idea what I was in for. But everything literally worked itself out piece by piece. I was even offered a place to stay in LA by complete strangers who had met me through a friend I was talking to on skype, that are now like my family.

People were so supportive and loving even though I did run into a rough patch; but then all of a sudden I ended up with my own place, I already had all my furniture. My son got to come home to his own room after a year of struggle; and my life simply restarts. Literally in months, I became a recognized celebrity photographer, motivational speaker, talk show host, producer, and now I'm writing this book! Can you guess why? The whispers in my spirit told me too. All I had to do was my part and follow through.

I don't know what happens from here. But what I do know, is that the whispers are never wrong. There's always a bigger picture. More times than not, it's bigger than any dream you could ever dream for yourself. When we fail to do the very thing that has been weighing heavy our heart and tugging at our spirit; we are unconsciously holding other people back. We are all chess pieces, shifting and moving into different places. Someone is waiting on you to do your part. Someone needs to see your work, hear your story or be inspired by something you have to give. That thing will create the spark they need to get moving in the right direction. Think about that as you procrastinate and continue to make excuses as to why you can't get it done or have the time. Finish what you've started, make time. Do your part, listen to your spirit. You never know how fast your life can change in every area you've been praying for. All you have to do is follow the whisper.

Chapter Twenty

THE POWER OF GRATITUDE

One of the greatest gifts you could ever give yourself or anyone else is the gift of Gratitude. I have watched my life completely transform in front of my eyes because I learned to simply be grateful for everything. When I wake up in the morning, that is the first thing that I do. I go through a mental gratitude list. I even have a gratitude jar as the first thing you see when you walk into my house. It's a neat way to incorporate your family and kids as well as sets the vibration for your home. My son and I write what we are grateful for on a little piece of paper every few days and at the end of the year, we count our blessings.

I read a passage somewhere that said, every day you should be grateful to the point of tears. And you know what, when I stop and say thank you; for all that I have, the amazing people in my life, the incredible opportunities I have, the support from people that believe in me, the gifts and talents I've been blessed with, the things I've survived, and the mind-blowing journey that I see foresee in the future. I immediately start tearing up. When you practice sincere Gratitude, you will begin to operate and manifest things on a level you can't even begin to comprehend because it's unimaginably magical.

Whenever I'm really down, depressed or when my financial flow has paused, and no money is coming in. I have found that it's because in some area of my life; I'm not being grateful enough. But the moment I catch myself and shift back into gratitude the flow opens right up. It seems like such a simple thing to do, but it takes a constant practice of compassion and being able to see the good in whatever situation you may be in. Gratitude will give you an effortless inner strength and peace that will draw people, situations, and opportunities to you like a magnet.

MANY of you don't even realize that you are so close to your breakthrough. But, you keep delaying your miracles when you vibrate at a low frequency by complaining, feeling as if the universe owes you something, bitter, stressed or constantly panicking about everything. You are creating the hell that you are stuck in. And you, can get yourself out. But you have to shift out of your comfort zone of misery, and move past the mindset of poverty and lack. Start expecting great things to happen. Step outside your little box and dream again. I am a believer of the impossible. The only limits you truly have, are the ones you set for yourself. I'm telling you, if you don't grab a hold of anything else in this book, you must get this.

I am challenging you to just try it for three days. And watch how the universe begins to open up blessings for you in ways you could never imagine.

Start by writing down at least five things you are grateful for everyday and 'WHY' as you say 'Thank you' after each one as many times as you want.

I personally stop most times and just get on my knees and say thank you over and over as I recount many things. And, even after I get up and take on my day, I still continue in that state of gratitude. This has helped me to be more calm, to flow through many challenges or obstacles and deal with people better overall. The more grateful I am, the more I receive to be grateful for.

Sometimes
we make choices in life, and
sometimes choices make
you.

Chapter Twenty One

DANCING IN THE RAIN

I received one of my greatest life lessons on the last day of my trip to Costa Rica while writing this book. I hadn't been to the ocean yet, so I decided that I would spend some time writing there. I wandered off and found a hidden beach surrounded by beautiful rocks in what looked to be a cove perfectly lined with trees and huge dark rocks along the edge. I caught a glimpse of it initially from the small trail where I was walking. It was absolutely breathtaking! I immediately whipped out my camera in an effort to capture the moment. I then wrote the word LIVE in the sand; that had clearly become the theme of my trip. I was learning to simply LIVE!

Suddenly, I felt tiny sprinkles of rain on my skin. Within seconds, those sprinkles turned into a full-blown thunderstorm. I hurried to put my camera away and ran to take cover. I became increasingly nervous as I frantically looked for a dry place to hide along the expanded strip of sand. There were lots of trees that could shelter me, but they were above these huge rocks that I wasn't prepared to climb (not in the slippery rain however.) Eventually, I spotted a branch that had fallen off one of the trees and I hid underneath it. As I crouched beneath the log, I heard the voice of a girl bursting with excitement and laughter. I peeked out to see what was happening; it was then that I saw a woman who appeared to be so full of life running topless into the ocean in the middle of the storm. I thought, WOW! That looks so fun, so carefree, so beautiful.

Her freedom seemed to rapidly liberate my soul. What was I hiding from? The rain? I mean I was in the middle of the freaking rain forest! What was there really to be afraid of in that moment? Regardless of the fact that I had a slight fear of drowning and knowing no one knew where I was; I desperately wanted to feel that type of freedom. So I said to myself, "I can do that!" I slowly but surely came out from beneath the branch that had given me comfort and safety from the storm. I took a deep breath, and walked straight into the ocean. I didn't care that I still had my clothes on, about my hair getting wet, or about what anyone else thought as they wondered what I was doing; as they also ran to take cover.

I walked further and further into the ocean until I came to a stop and just stood there. I closed my eyes and lifted my head to the sky while being completely drenched by the rain. As it rushed down my face; I began to feel the sand moving underneath my feet. I felt myself grounding and becoming more aware, as I could feel everything. It was almost as if I was being cleansed by the heavens. I opened my eyes to what looked like an entirely different place while I stood chest length in the ocean. Everything suddenly became so calm, although the storm still raged. My body began to feel warmer; as if the water had heated up just for me. I wasn't shivering at all anymore. The colors of the ocean, and the trees appeared so vivid and bright like they had come alive from where I was standing. It was so fascinating.

I thought back to where I had been hiding underneath the branch, and how from there everything looked so dark, cloudy & dingy. There was no color, no sunlight, nothing. But here, standing in the midst of the storm the view was magical, not at all like what I envisioned.

Then I had another Aha moment as I began to laugh at myself out loud, while I spun around with my arms spread wide and lifting my face to the sky. I felt so free. Gratitude washed over me, and I simply said, "Thank you. I get it now! I get it.... Thank you"

I had been so afraid of the unknown that I almost missed out on one of the most beautiful and life changing moments I have ever experienced. I had been conditioned to hide from the rain, not run into it. But, it felt so good; even though I was drenched from head to toe; and probably looking a hot mess. I felt alive and beautiful. I was able to experience the true meaning of bliss – pure and unconditional joy and peace - as I laughed out loud to myself. I realized there was nothing to honestly fear at all. I decided to just live, be present and embrace every moment.

DO what you feel. Don't be afraid to try new things that others are afraid to do, no matter what they may think or say, because you may miss out on something amazing. What looked so scary - that massive ocean; could not have been more comforting, more peaceful, more beautiful or more cleansing to my soul. I realized what looked so frightening from the outside, was actually not at all, it didn't hurt me nor was it trying to. It actually felt amazing. Perception can often be deceiving; which limits us from experiencing something we've been conditioned to believe is bad or wrong. Deceptive perception can embed fear into our DNA, which we inadvertently pass along to each generation; continuing to hold one another back from reaching our full potential; all because of fearing the unknown.

NO matter what you're going through, no matter how foreign the territory may seem, or whatever fear you've been conditioned to use as excuses because of what life has thrown at you, just go out there and dance honey! It's much more magnificent than you could ever imagine. Surrendering to the unknown - that is how you *Redefine Strong.*

At the end of
my life, I want
to be able to say
I did more than
just exist. I
lived!

— Phoenix White

My Gratitude List

I just wanted to take a moment to thank some of the incredible people that have helped to change my life in so many ways. Without them, this book would not have been possible.

God | My Guides | My Angels | Holy Spirit | My Ancestors
Thank you for guiding and protecting me throughout this journey. Thank you for keeping me safe and helping to get through so much. Thank you choosing me to be a servant of humanity, to help heal, inspire and empower people. I know that I am just a vessel and that it's bigger than me. Thank you for healing and abundance in every area of my life. Thank you for giving me strength when I didn't think I was going to make it. Thank you for helping me to get through this book. I know I fought it early on. But I am so grateful as the process has taught me so much. Thank you Thank you Thank you... For everything.

My Mom
I don't even know where to start. We've been through so much. Without your support and sacrifice to help keep my life together where ever I fell short, I don't know if I would have made it this far. This book would not have been possible without you. You are an absolutely amazing person. Thank you for always showing up and showing out as we say. LOL. Thank you for having my back in everything I do, and supporting every dream I believe in. Thank you for instilling the spirit of excellence in me. Thank you for teaching me about God. Thank you for passing your strength to me as a woman with grace and power. THANK YOU for being my backbone and best friend. You are irreplaceable. I love you.

My Dad

Thank you for always having my back. I learned how to work hard from you. Thank you for always being a great dad. Thank you for constantly being straight up with me and always having my back. Thank you for always answering the phone whenever I needed you, and for always making it easy for me to be honest with you growing up. You are a great dad. Thank you for never leaving your kids. You are one of my best friends and I love you more than you know.

Jonathan Harris

Wow... I would've never thought when I stumbled across your class on meet up a few years ago that my life would change forever. Thank you for allowing God to use you to catapult me into my true calling and purpose. Without you guiding and helping me to clear my path and teaching me how to truly tap into my spiritual gifts, there would absolutely be no book. Thank you for always being honest and true to yourself. You've taught me so much. Thank you for being such a good friend. I love and appreciate you so much. Without you, I would not be where I am today.

My Besties: Janell & Ghia

What can I say, you guys have been my best friends for over 13 years. You guys know all my business... My flaws, my strengths, my joys, my pain. But you both have always stayed the same. Thank you guys for never leaving me, even when I was so lost. You never changed and you never made me feel judged. You were both right there at my bedside every time I was in the hospital, praying for me and making me laugh.

Because of you both I know what true friendship looks and feels like. Thank you for loving and believing in me.

Aunt Tonya

You are such a pillar of strength. I want to thank you for always having my back. Because of you, I was able to go to Costa Rica and start this book. You pushed me to do it even when I didn't think I was good enough or ready. Thank you for all the nights you stayed up with me. All the court hearings you sat in, and all the hospital rooms you slept in with me as you prayed & believed for me through it all. It's been a long road, but it's finally here. I couldn't have done it without you. I'm so grateful you're in my life and I love you so much. The train has left the station. LOL

Lamman Rucker

Thank you for being one of my best friends for the last 10 years. I have learned so much from you. Thank you for always challenging me to grow; in character, in conversation, in my thinking. Thank you for always being my voice of reason and for taking on so much of my heaviness over the years and helping me to sort it out without you getting overwhelmed. Thank you for being the man my son looks up to and models himself after. Had not you stepped in. I don't know where I would be mentally and emotionally, even to this day. Thank you for being a great 'God Dad' to the midget and always being there; especially when it matters most. Thank you for being a leader and example for so many young boys including. You are one of the bests gifts I could've ever been given. Because of you, my son has never truly felt the void of a father. Thank you for teaching me how to be a great mother to a son, when I had no idea what I was doing. Also, thank you for being an example of what it means to give back to help inspire other. You started me on that path. Thank you for teaching me how to slow down and be present. I love you. I appreciate you. Thank you.

Tyrese Gibson

We haven't spoken in a while since my days as your recording artist up at HQ. But I want you to know that I have been watching, following & supporting you from a distance. Your transformation is so Powerful. I want you to know that you have inspired me beyond measure. I am so grateful for your knowledge, raw honesty and your ability to articulate things in a way that have rapidly lifted my soul and consciousness. So I just want you to know that you have changed my life. Keep making those videos. You are empowering more people than you know. I am one of them.

Oprah Winfrey

Thank you for providing a woman of color like me an example of what it means to walk in the true fulfillment of purpose. There has not been one instance that I walked away from anything you have been apart of without having a life changing experience or 'Aha' moment. It was you that I looked to that kept me on track and inspired me to rise up out of many dark places. I know I will meet you one day. But I just wanted you to know that without you, I wouldn't be possible and neither would this book. Thank you for teaching me how to Redefine

Strong. You have and continue to change my life and for that I am eternally grateful to you. Not only have you answered and accepted your call. You have taught and inspired us all to do the same. Thank you, Thank you, Thank you!

Iyanla Vanzant

My spiritual teacher from afar! You have literally shifted the entire core of my being. It was you that taught me to dig deep into my stuff and do the work needed to move me out of pain and into greatness. I am eternally grateful as you have been and continue to be the kick in the butt that makes me jump up out of pity and own and acknowledge my participation in my pain. Which includes my mistakes, shame and the guilt that was ruining my life. Thank you for giving me the prescription for healing and the blueprint for putting my house back together. Thank you, thank you, thank you.

Kevonne Spaulding

My spiritual sister... Giiiiirrrlllll you don't know how much I appreciate you. Thank you for teaching me what it means to be a healer and for listening to every crazy question or experience I had as I learned how to attune to this new awakening. Thank you for understanding me and being right there during this process helping me through it. Thank you for guiding me and helping me to trust my inner voice. As well as sometimes being the only person I could tell certain things to without making me feel shame, guilt or insane. You are an amazing light worker and friend. It was you who even stayed up with me to the late hours so that I could finish this book by my due date. I'm so grateful you're in my life. Xoxo

Anthony Hamilton

You have been one of my best friends for over 10 years. Thank you for helping me to heal by sharing your incredible love and light with me. Thank you for always building me up and helping me to grow into a woman that I love. Thank you for seeing greatness in me when I didn't see it in myself. Thank you for showing me my true beauty, brilliance and light without all the stuff. Thank for charging my spiritual battery when it was dead and for always keeping me safe. Thank you for never changing and having pure motives and intentions. You're an amazing friend, I love you.

To all of my Sisters and Brothers

Jenea, Brittany, Jamila, Jeston & Jesse. I love you guys. Thank you for being my biggest supporters. To all my cousins, aunts, and uncles. I Love you all - there's too many of you to write individually because you guys will get upset if I forget one of you. Xoxo

My Supporters

To everyone on social media, and most that I have never met or seen that continually lift me up with encouragement, support and prayers; Thank you.... I see all of your comments, reposts, and likes. I also feel your prayers. I am so inspired by many of you. You guys kept me going many days without even knowing. My prayer is that this book empowers, inspires and evokes healing in your lives. I pray special blessings and favor over all of you. Thank you, Thank you, Thank you!

My Angels in Disguise

Although I won't remember everyone. I do want to say thank you to some amazing people in my life. Many are Angels is disguise that have helped, supported and believed in me. I love you guys!! These names are 'in no particular order whatsoever.'
THANK YOU WITH ALL MY HEART!

Valarie Edwards
Kimm Epps
Velisa Crayton-Walker
Natasha Ellie
Stephanie Owens
Marie Thomas
Lillie Argulard
Meiko Drew
Tinesia Conwright
DB Woodside
John Salley
Stephanie Solomon-Brown
Caleb Henderson
Brandon Lee Anderson
Corey Reese
Pat O'Brien
Pierre Conley
Jeff Johnson
Chris Hicks
Danielle Dredden
Annette Bibbey-Oliver
Grandma Daisy Woodfolk
Lydia Cincore-Templeton
Gwendolyn Taylor

Keite Young
B Slade
Andrew Glassman
Aaron Long
Aja Franks
Linda Torrence
Derrick Clark
Sky Heavens
Cat Wilson
Maile & Bill Fernandez
Olana Himmel
Logan Alexander
Roderick Pinkney
Star Johnson
Kemic Smothers
Chuck Harmony
Craig 'Boogie' Stocks
Spicy Mari
Natasha Robb
Mama Bessie
Stephanie Fleitas
Necee Wilson
Yesenia Gutierrez
Malik Whitfield

Robyn Williams
Antonique Smith
Adrian & LaDedra Ewings
David Simmons
Mena Wright
Iyana Wright
Shantee Wright
Horace Blenman
Ken Joseph
Sharon Black
Renae Tyler

REDEFINING

Thank you for reading.
I would love for you to keep in touch.
Xo ~Phoenix

 phoenixwhite

 phoenixontwit

 phoenixwhite

 phoenixwhite

 info@phoenixwhite.net

phoenixwhite.net

Made in the USA
San Bernardino, CA
23 February 2015